Twayne's English Authors Series

EDITOR OF THIS VOLUME

Bertram H. Davis

The Florida State University

Samuel Foote

TEAS 284

Samuel Foote

SAMUEL FOOTE

By ELIZABETH N. CHATTEN

Rose Bruford College, London

TWAYNE PUBLISHERS

A DIVISION OF G. K. HALL & CO., BOSTON

Copyright © 1980 by G. K. Hall & Co.

Published in 1980 by Twayne Publishers,
A Division of G. K. Hall & Co.
All Rights Reserved

Printed on permanent/durable acid-free paper and bound
in the United States of America
First Printing

Library of Congress Cataloging in Publication Data

Chatten, Elizabeth N
Samuel Foote.

(Twayne's English authors series; TEAS 284)
Bibliography: p. 153–57
Includes index.
1.–Foote, Samuel, 1720–1777—
Criticism and interpretation.
PR3461.F6C5   822'.6   79-21394
ISBN 0-8057-6779-7

Contents

About the Author

Elizabeth Chatten was born in Canada and now lives in Great Britain. After completing B.A. and M.A. studies at the University of Calgary she was in 1970 awarded a Canada Council Fellowship which financed four years of research in England, where she pursued her interests in theater and theater history. Ms. Chatten lectures in drama and theater studies at Rose Bruford College in London.

Preface

Although now better known to modern readers through Boswell's *Life of Johnson* than the more than twenty of his published two- and three-act plays, Samuel Foote remains a fascinating figure in eighteenth-century theater history. Like many later critics, Johnson could not bring himself to approve of Foote's reliance on mimicry, caricature, and personal satire, nor could he keep from laughing at Foote's wit. Despite the fact that the prolific Foote's plays were not considered "regular" comedy, he succeeded in drawing large audiences throughout his thirty-year career as actor, manager, and playwright. His success alone warrants an examination of his works in the context of the eighteenth-century tradition of the afterpiece.

Foote is in many ways the representative eighteenth-century man. Well-born but slightly eccentric, he was a brilliant conversationalist in an era noted for wit. He parlayed his talent for mimicry into an acting career and from his seemingly inexhaustible wit drew material for his plays. Reading these plays, one is struck by Foote's surprising modernity. His dramatic satires are closely akin to satirical revue and to television situation comedy. Critics in the eighteenth century tended to derogate Foote, suggesting that, like Mac Flecknoe, he "promis'd a play, and dwindled to a farce." But Foote always maintained that his writing was patterned on the satiric Old Comedy of ancient Greece, and his plays contain both personal and social satire. Like his contemporary, Hogarth, he looked at society with a critical, penetrating eye. The comprehensiveness of Foote's satire gives his works unique value for the social historian, while his choice of the satiric mode places him firmly within eighteenth-century literary tradition.

Foote believed that comedy should seek to correct the absurdities and vices of society, and I intend to consider him primarily as a social satirist. His comedies attack a wide variety of social evils and ridicule individual foibles, and because he acted in many of his own plays he was able to use his talent as a natural mimic in support of his own satire. One of the problems in assessing Foote's plays, however, has been to decide where he only mimics, and where his mimicry becomes imitation of a type rather than of an individual. Contemporary audiences recognized with delight the personal allusions, but later readers can see in Foote's characters representations of a more typical nature.

Increased interest in Foote points to a recognition of his significance. Benjamin Blom recently has reprinted the two-volume *Works* of 1809 and Foote's *Treatise on the Passions* [1747], while the first scholarly treatment of the plays, Mary Megie Belden's *The Dramatic Work of Samuel Foote*, was reprinted by Archon Books in 1970. Simon Trefman's biography, *Sam. Foote, Comedian, 1720–1777*, appeared in 1971. In 1973, two hundred years after its initial performance, Foote's *Piety in Pattens* was published for the first time in an admirable critical edition by Samuel N. Bogorad and Robert Gale Noyes, an achievement which highlights the need for a similar treatment of Foote's other comedies.

With Foote's plays now easily available, it is hoped that this study of his works may provide a critical appreciation of his dramatic satire, and of his place in eighteenth-century theater history. Foote's wit, his flair for reproducing characteristic dialogue, and his unerring delineation of the ludicrous and predatory elements in his society make him worthy of attention. His portraits of his contemporaries can still provide much pleasure. Unfortunately, Foote's reputation as a clever mimic and bon vivant, the "incompressible fellow" who won Johnson's reluctant admiration, has led in the past to a criticism of his work characterized by a strange blend of aesthetic and moral disapproval, and part of the task necessary in evaluating the plays is to look at them objectively in the light of social history. Sometimes Foote's life and his writing converge, and biographical details illuminate the plays. A sense of his importance should, however, be based on a consideration of his achievement as a dramatic satirist, a writer of Old Comedy, rather than on the usual critical comparison of Foote to other authors who wrote in comic modes he did not attempt. In general, therefore, I concentrate on discussion of his dramatic works and of his essays on comedy and tragedy.

In the absence of critical editions of Foote's plays I have for the sake of easy reference taken all quotations from the only edition of his *Works* currently in print. This is a reprint of the 1809 two-volume edition, which contains only minor variations from the first editions, or first authorized editions. I am indebted to Professor Samuel N. Bogorad, of the University of Vermont, for providing me with copies of the Huntington Library and the Folger Library manuscripts of *Piety in Patterns*, and for permission to quote from his edition of this play.

ELIZABETH N. CHATTEN

Rose Bruford College, London

Chronology

1721   Samuel Foote born in Truro, Cornwall; baptized January 27.

1737   June 29, admitted to Worcester College, Oxford.

1740   February 25, scholarship revoked as a result of frequent unexplained absences from Worcester College.

1741   January 10, marries Mary Hickes, at St. Clements, near Truro, Cornwall.

1744   February 6, acting debut, playing Othello to Charles Macklin's Iago at the Haymarket Theatre.

1744–1745   Acts at Smock Alley Theatre, Dublin.

1745–1746   Acts at Drury Lane Theatre.

1747   Publishes *A Treatise on the Passions, So far as they regard the Stage*, and *The Roman and English Comedy Consider'd and Compar'd*. April 22, *The Diversions of the Morning* produced at the Haymarket Theatre.

1748   April 18, *An Auction of Pictures* produced at the Haymarket Theatre.

1749   April 3, *The Knights* produced at the Haymarket Theatre.

1752   January 11, *Taste* produced at Drury Lane Theatre.

1753   March 24, *The Englishman in Paris* produced at Covent Garden Theatre.

1756   February 3, *The Englishman Return'd from Paris* produced at Covent Garden Theatre.

1757   February 5, *The Author* produced at Drury Lane Theatre.

1760   January 28, *The Minor* produced at the Crow Street Theatre, Dublin. June 28, first London performance of *The Minor* at the Haymarket Theatre.

1761   April 6, *Tragedy a la Mode* produced at Drury Lane Theatre.

1762   January 12, *The Lyar* produced at Covent Garden Theatre. April 28, *The Orators* produced at the Haymarket Theatre.

1763   May 11, *The Trial of Samuel Foote* . . . produced at the Haymarket Theatre. June 20, *The Mayor of Garratt* produced at the Haymarket Theatre.

1764   June 13, *The Patron* produced at the Haymarket Theatre.

1765   June 10, *The Commissary* produced at the Haymarket Theatre.

1766   Accident on February 3 leads to the amputation of Foote's leg. July 5, granted a Royal patent for a summer theater.

1767   May 29, opens refurbished Haymarket Theatre with the first performance of *An Occasional Prelude*.

1768   May 30, *The Devil Upon Two Sticks* produced at the Haymarket Theatre.

1770   June 22, *The Lame Lover* produced at the Haymarket Theatre.

1771   June 26, *The Maid of Bath* produced at the Haymarket Theatre.

1772   June 29, *The Nabob* produced at the Haymarket Theatre.

1773   February 15, *Piety in Pattens* produced at the Haymarket Theatre. July 21, *The Bankrupt* produced at the Haymarket Theatre.

1774   July 15, *The Cozeners* produced at the Haymarket Theatre.

1775   *A Trip to Calais* refused a license by the Lord Chamberlain.

1776   August 19, *The Capuchin* produced at the Haymarket Theatre. December 15, Foote acquitted of a charge of homosexual assault.

1777   January 16, Foote's interest in the Haymarket Theatre sold to George Colman the Elder. The sale had been agreed to in October, 1776, but was not announced until after Foote's trial. Death of Foote at the Ship Inn, Dover, on October 21. Burial in Westminster Abbey on October 27.

CHAPTER 1

Foote and the Theatrical Milieu

I *Extravagance and Eccentricity*

SAMUEL Foote, actor, wit, and dramatist, was born in Truro, Cornwall, in 1721.[1] His parents, Samuel and Eleanor Foote, were persons of some standing in the community, his father having been Member of Parliament for Tiverton, Commissioner of the Prize Office and Receiver of Fines for the Duchy, as well as Mayor of Truro for a time. Apparently Foote senior also served as a justice, and William Cooke, Foote's friend and biographer, in his *Memoirs of Samuel Foote* recounts an early instance of young Samuel's talent for mimicry, when at the age of eleven or twelve he entertained his parents' dinner guests with imitations of his father and the other justices.[2]

Foote's mother, the former Eleanor Goodere, was the only daughter of Sir Edward Goodere. She eventually inherited a considerable fortune through the death of her brother, Sir John Dinely Goodere, who was murdered in 1740 by another brother, Captain Samuel Goodere. Young Samuel Foote, by this time a man-about-town in London, is said by Cooke[3] to have earned ten pounds with a broadsheet entitled the *Genuine Memoirs of Sir John Dinely Goodere, Bart., who was murdered by the Contrivance of his Own Brother on Board the Ruby Man of War in King's Road, near Bristol, Jan. 19, 1740. Together with the Life History and Last Dying Words of his Brother, Captain Samuel Goodere, who was executed at Bristol on the 15th day of April, 1741, for the Horrid Murder of the said Sir J. D. Goodere. Dedicated to the Rt. Worshipful H. Combe, Mayor of Bristol. By S. Foote, of Worcester College, Oxford, etc.,* and nephew to the late Sir John D. Goodere. The crime gained for Foote a degree of notoriety. Samuel Johnson related that Cooke "presented Foote to a Club, in the following singular manner: 'This is the nephew of the gentleman who was lately hung in chains for

murdering his brother.' "[4] Foote's early venture into print, on a
subject of domestic scandal and concern which anyone else would
have wished suppressed, reveals his ability to capitalize upon matters of public interest, as well as that opportunism and impudence
with which he has often been charged.

The unfortunate Sir John Dinely Goodere was noted for his eccentricities, and his sister, Mrs. Foote, seems in some measure to
have shared this family trait. Like her son, she was extravagant and
irrepressible. When Cooke met her, she was seventy-nine and as
active as a woman of forty. He found her "witty, humorous, and
convivial".[5] Cooke quotes as evidence of their improvidence and
extravagance the following exchange between mother and son:

DEAR SAM,
I AM in prison for debt: come and assist your loving mother,

E. FOOTE

DEAR MOTHER,
SO am I; which prevents his duty being paid to his loving mother by her
affectionate son,

SAM. FOOTE

P.S. I have sent my attorney to assist you; in the mean time let us hope
for better days.[6]

As well as having a gift for repartee when *in extremis*, Foote was
a brilliant conversationalist. Charles Cowden Clarke, writing in *The
Gentleman's Magazine* almost a hundred years after Foote's death,
pays tribute to the actor's reputation for wit and learning: "He was
well educated, and was a variously read man; and report says of
him, that in the thick of the most thoughtless mad waggery, he
could upon a sudden change of subject, discourse with sedateness
upon the philosophy of history, upon politics, and upon classical
and general learning."[7] Only Garrick, and possibly Arthur Murphy,
among the members of the theatrical profession, could vie with
Foote as a scholar, and contemporary accounts are virtually unan-
imous in granting Foote superiority in wit. Samuel Johnson's evaluation of the two famous actor-managers is a case in point:

Dr. Johnson compared the different talents of Garrick and Foote, as com panions, and gave Garrick greatly the preference for elegance, though he allowed Foote extraordinary powers of entertainment. He said, "Garrick is restrained by some principle; but Foote has the advantage of an unlimited range. Garrick has some delicacy of feeling; it is possible to put him out; you may get the better of him; but Foote is the most incompressible fellow that I ever knew: when you have driven him into a corner, and think you are sure of him, he runs through between your legs, or jumps over your head, and makes his escape.[8]

This same resourceful wit was to be invaluable in getting Foote out of the difficult situations in which some of his plays embroiled him.

A gentleman by birth, and a wit by nature, Samuel Foote owed what scholarly attributes he possessed to his education at Worcester Grammar School and Worcester College, Oxford. He left Oxford February 25, 1740, without taking a degree, reportedly because of his wild pranks and disregard for the college rules. After leaving Oxford, Foote apparently intended to study law at the Inner Temple, but as his name is not to be found on the Temple's lists, it is likely that at most he merely lodged there.[9] Within a year of leaving Oxford, Foote married, although little is known of his wife except for her name, Mary Hickes, and the fact that she was heir to some property in Cornwall.[10] Their married life as revealed in various anecdotes cannot have been happy, though as these stories all turn on jests made by Foote at his wife's expense, perhaps she was the chief sufferer, as the butt of his cruel wit. Although she lived with Foote in London she seems to have taken little part in his social life. Foote quickly was accepted among the London coffeehouse wits, but his extravagant way of life eventually exhausted his "considerable fortune," if not his spirits, and he turned to the stage for a living.

II *The Theatrical Milieu*

In the early 1740s, London theatrical activity was largely confined to the two patent houses. The Licensing Act of June 21, 1737, not only had placed the licensing of plays under the jurisdiction of the Lord Chamberlain but had prohibited the performance of plays at any location not sanctioned by a Royal patent, as was Covent Garden, or licensed by the Lord Chamberlain, as was Drury Lane.[11] The minor theaters, such as Goodman's Fields and the Little Theatre in the Haymarket (where Fielding's plays had been performed) had to close, at least for a time. Various actors and managers attempted theatrical performances in contravention of the Act. Some performed unmolested; but other performances were prohibited, and one manager, James Lacy, was temporarily imprisoned. Such entertainments as puppet shows, pantomimes, concerts, and orations, however, not being considered legitimate drama, were permitted. This situation led to many attempts at evading the law through the use of what came to be known as the "concert" formula, in which a concert was advertised, together with a note that a comedy would be performed, gratis, during the intermission. Theatrical promoters utilized this device to produce plays at the minor theaters and at booths during fair days. In addition, the Lord Chamberlain occasionally granted licenses for special performances. Arthur H. Scouten, writing in *The London Stage* (an indispensable reference work for students of the period) on the effects of the Licensing Act, points out that the Lord Chamberlain was more vigorous and efficient in censoring plays than in prohibiting performances in unlicensed theaters.[12] The government succeeded in its aim of prohibiting the acting of plays containing any political satire, but apparently tolerated many politically innocuous unlicensed performances. Meanwhile the two licensed houses enjoyed a virtual monopoly and prospered accordingly.

An evening at the playhouse during the eighteenth century included a variety of entertainments. A prologue was generally followed by a five-act mainpiece, an epilogue, a theatrical dance, and a two-act afterpiece, together with popular music and specialty acts such as tumbling and slackwire performances.[13] The repertory included, in addition to new plays, Elizabethan and Jacobean drama, with an emphasis on Shakespeare and Jonson, and revivals of comedies of manners as well as the popular sentimental comedy. Afterpieces were generally farcical in nature. When Foote later began to perform in his own two- and three-act comedies at the Haymarket, those which were particularly successful often served as afterpieces at one of the patent houses in the subsequent winter season.

III *Foote's Acting Debut*

On February 6, 1744, Foote made his acting debut, playing Othello to Charles Macklin's Iago at the Haymarket. Macklin had

evaded the Licensing Act by advertising that *Othello* "will be perform'd by a set of Gentlemen for their own Diversion, no money
will be taken at the Doors nor any person admitted but by printed
Tickets; which will be deliver'd gratis by Mr. Macklin at his House
in Bow Street, Covent Garden."[14] The authorities soon stopped the
play, but in any case Foote was no success as a tragedian. Cooke
quotes Macklin's description of the performance:

It was little better than a total failure; that . . . [Foote's] singling out this
part was much against . . . [Macklin's] judgment, as neither his figure,
voice, nor manners, corresponded with the character; and in those mixed
passages of *tenderness* and *rage*, the former was expressed so *whiningly*,
and the latter in a tone so *sharp* and *inharmonious*, that the audience could
scarcely refrain from laughing. Not [added Macklin] but one could plainly
discover the scholar about the young man, and that he perfectly knew what
the author meant; but in the exhibition of the passions (where nature alone
must be the tutor) he was miserably defective.[15]

Despite this inauspicious beginning, Foote acted in the winter
of 1744–1745 at the Smock Alley Theatre in Dublin, where Thomas
Sheridan was manager, and the following winter became a member
of the regular Drury Lane company. He seems to have played comic
roles exclusively. In Vanbrugh's *Relapse* he acted Lord Foppington
to Peg Woffington's Berinthia and Kitty Clive's Miss Hoyden, and,
in Farquhar's *Constant Couple*, Sir Harry Wildair to Woffington's
Lady Lurewell. Other roles included Sir Novelty Fashion in Cib-
ber's *Love's Last Shift*, Sir Courtly Nice in Crowne's comedy of that
name, and Dick in Vanbrugh's *Confederacy*, but his greatest
triumph was as Bayes in Buckingham's *The Rehearsal*. Character-
istically, as Bayes, Foote used his talent for mimicry to "take off"
the leading actors of the day. This was not an innovation, Garrick
having used the role of Bayes for the same purpose when he played
at Goodman's Fields in 1741–1742;[16] but the use of *The Rehearsal*
to satirize contemporary actors added a new dimension to the play,
fulfilling the spirit of Buckingham's entertainment while making it
relevant to the 1740s. Bayes was always one of Foote's favorite roles,
and in his treatment *The Rehearsal* became a kind of revue: an old
play was turned into a new event. John Genest, in his stage history
of the period, reports on a performance in 1776:

Aug. 2. Foote acted Bayes—his performance in this part was an odd mixture of his own dialogue and that of the original piece, which he contrived to make coalesce as well as he could—his fancy was so exuberant, his conceptions so ready, and his thoughts so brilliant, that he kept the audience in continual laughter—public transactions, the flying follies of the day, debates in grave assemblies, absurdities of play-writers, politicians and players, all came under his cognizance and all felt the force of his wit; in short he laid hold of every thing and every body, that would furnish materials for the evening.[17]

Foote's and Garrick's imitations of the actors were thus extremely topical. Acting techniques in the mid-eighteenth century were in a state of transition, and a theatergoer often could see the old and the new methods coexisting rather uneasily within the same play. Older actors like Quin tended toward rhetorical declamation, but Macklin and Garrick both favored a more natural and realistic delivery. As Garrick rose to prominence as the leading actor and manager of his age, his style was almost universally adopted. It was particularly well suited to the relatively small theaters of the day: Drury Lane's capacity at that time was 1800, and Covent Garden's 1400,[18] even when spectators were crowded onto benches in the pit. The size of the playhouses and the good lighting permitted close observation, and contemporary accounts describe the audiences' attentiveness to Garrick's facial expressions. This is the type of "intimate theater" in which Samuel Foote worked as actor and manager in the Garrick era, and to which he brought his genius for low comedy and mimicry.

IV First Plays

Foote was not in sufficient demand as an actor to support his extravagant manner of living, and he turned in 1747 to writing his own plays, which provided vehicles for his ability as a mimic. With characteristic ingenuity, he varied the "concert" formula in advertising his performances, and has a place in theatrical history as one of the most successful evaders of the Licensing Act. An attempted evening performance of his first play, *The Diversions of the Morning*, having been forbidden by the authorities, Foote advertised subsequent performances for noonday. Public breakfastings, auctions, and boxing matches were commonly held at this hour, and by calling his productions variously "a dish of chocolate," "a dish of tea," or "an auction of pictures," and not naming the play to be performed, Foote managed to continue his performances.[19] In addition, he took advantage of the "puff," the insertion of notices about plays into the news columns. Scouten has noted that Foote also got free publicity by "planting" in the newspapers letters calculated to create controversy: "On 20 April 1747, at the beginning of the season at the New Haymarket, the *Daily Advertiser* carried an angry response in which Foote is threatened with horsewhipping if he puts on his show. On the next day Orator Henley paid two shillings for a notice in the *General Advertiser* entitled 'Foote a Fool,' in which he attacked Foote in his usual vigorous and coarse manner. Henley normally advertised only in the *Daily Advertiser;* by being trapped into attacking Foote in the other paper he simply saved Foote two shillings."[20] The first plays that Foote wrote and presented at the Haymarket in the spring of 1747 are better described as revues than comedies. Tate Wilkinson described *The Diversions of the Morning* as "principally made up of satirical mimicry of actors, such as Quin, Delane, Ryan, Woodward, Mrs. Woffington, and of Garrick, upon whom he was especially severe."[21] Apparently Foote's style of mimicry included both visual and vocal imitation, as Cooke's remarks upon the same play indicate: "This piece consisted of nothing more than the introduction of several well-known characters in real life, whose manner of conversation and expression this author had very happily hit in the diction of his drama, and still more happily represented on the stage, by an exact imitation, not only of the manner and tone of voice, but even of the very persons of those whom he intended *to take off.*"[22]

Also on the program was a farce adapted from the *Old Bachelor*, called the *Credulous Husband*, in which Foote played Fondlewife.[23] It became fashionable to attend his matinees, and his clever mimicry was soon the talk of the town. However, Foote did not rely solely on himself and his fellow actors to entertain the audience, but regularly employed dancers to provide variety in his program.[24] Often these dancers were students whom he could engage at low rates. By June 1, 1747, he had put back the hour of his entertainment to 6:30 P.M., the usual time of performances at the patent houses. His "Tea" on June 6, 1747, is billed as "the 35th day and positively the last,"[25] indicating that his performance had been given an average of five days out of every seven for a six-week period, a spectacular run in that era, when the average tenure of a play was nine or ten nights, and fifteen was unusual.[26] Similar revues and farces were produced by Foote and his company until the spring of 1749 when his first regular comedy, *The Knights,* appeared.

Cooke tells of an encounter relating to the production of "Tea" between Foote and Quin. It reveals Foote's recurring financial difficulties, and suggests also some degree of animosity on the part of Quin, one of those actors "taken off" in the play:

When Quin first heard of Foote's success in *giving tea* at the Haymarket, he said, in his sarcastical manner, "he was glad of it; for now, poor devil! we may expect to see him with a clean shirt on." Foote, hearing of this, charged him one night at the Bedford with taking such a liberty with him, as to say "he should now wear *clean shirts.*"—"No, Sir," says Quin, very gravely, "I did not say *shirts,* I said *shirt*: when I spoke of you on this subject, I could not be so *ignorant* as to use the *plural number.*"[27]

Foote operated the Little Theatre in the Haymarket intermittently from 1747 until 1766, usually employing about twelve actors. When he was granted a patent for a summer theater in 1766, he expanded his acting company and commenced regular operation for an allowed fifty-two performances a season. Foote's profitable summer runs continued until he sold his patent and retired from management at the end of 1776.

Although a spendthrift in personal life, Foote was an astute theatrical manager. He opened the theater an average of three days a week, and kept his acting requirements to a minimum by limiting his repertory and often taking several roles in a play himself. Even his enlarged company typically included only twenty-one actors, ten actresses, and four dancers.[28] Foote's repertoire, nicely calculated to attract summer audiences, is described in *The London Stage*: "Occasionally he essayed a play familiar in the repertory of the patent theatres—a *Beggar's Opera,* a *Rehearsal,* or even *She Stoops to Conquer* and *Richard III*, perhaps a musical such as *Love in a Village.* But his staple for his allowable fifty-two performances usually involved a dozen light mainpieces accompanied by about eighteen different afterpieces, interspersed with mimicry. . . . He often brought out two or three of his own new pieces each summer, which were later sheered [sic] down to afterpieces for the patent theatres the following season."[29] Foote's program provided light entertainment for the summer season, and did not greatly encroach upon the repertory of the patent theaters.

V *Scandal and Society*

What Foote had done was to find a larger, paying audience for the kind of wit and mimicry he habitually dispensed *gratis* at the Bedford Coffee House or the homes of his aristocratic friends. At the beginning of his career he was less a dramatist than what might be termed a literary personality. Foote himself was more than somewhat eccentric, and it is paradoxical that his plays are in many instances based on the eccentricities of others.

There is an element of the preposterous in his most amusing characterizations, evidence of his idiosyncratic wit. But London society in the latter half of the eighteenth century abounded with eccentrics, whose antics are described with delicious malice in Horace Walpole's *Letters*. T. H. White calls his appropriately gossipy study of the period *The Age of Scandal*. White is exceptionally good at conjuring up the flavor of that intimate, aristocratic society in which Foote lived, and which he recreated in comically transmuted form on the stage:

Few people seem to realize how charming and peculiar the Age of Scandal was. We have to dismiss so much from our minds before we can crawl inside theirs: before we can picture the powdered gentlemen in silks and laces, with their jewellery and the swords which they were ready to draw, with their sedan chairs and lap dogs and immense potations. . . . They were emotional about their friends, catty about their enemies, unusual in their hobbies, and singular in themselves. They were perhaps the first people in English literature to be real enough for gossip.

Gossip must be about character. It is useless to gossip about an unknown character, impossible to tell a good story about a person without foibles; for it is the foible which gives the story point. These people had characters, were among the first people in England who were sufficiently peculiar, in a modern way, to be apprehended by us as personalities.[30]

Foote's dramatic satires, peopled with real and imaginary eccentric characters, are images of this society.

Foote acquired his patent in a peculiar manner. In 1766, he was one of a party visiting Lord Mexborough's estate and, being dared to ride a spirited horse, was thrown and his leg so badly fractured as to require amputation. The Duke of York, also one of the party, obtained for Foote a lifetime patent enabling him to erect a theater in the city and liberties of Westminster, and present dramatic entertainments during the season from May 14 to September 14. Foote bought and refurbished the Haymarket, and entered into a ten-year period of prosperity. Having begun by evading the Licensing Act, he became, through the loss of his leg, a patentee, one of only three in London. From 1766 onward drama could legitimately be presented at Covent Garden, Drury Lane and, in the summer, at the Haymarket.

CHAPTER 2

Early Plays: Theory and Practice

I Revue and Revenge

OF Foote's earlier plays the only surviving fragments are the second act of *The Diversions of the Morning*, as performed at Drury Lane in 1758–1759, and the 1761 replacement of act 2, *Tragedy a-la-Mode.*[1] But, judging from contemporary reports, the early plays consisted chiefly of satirical revue and caricature. Foote's mimicry of the actors in *The Diversions of the Morning* has been noted in chapter 1. Frequent changes in the targets of his satire are attested to by alterations in the advertisement, "which would call attention to 'a new character' or 'a new dessert' to be offered at the *Tea*, or 'some originals by a new master' at the *Auction.*"[2] One of the "originals" delineated by Foote in his *Auction of Pictures* (April 18, 1748) was Henry Fielding. The warfare of these two wits is described at length by Martin C. Battestin in his "Fielding and 'Master Punch' in Panton Street."[3] Fielding's puppet show in Panton Street competed with Foote's noonday entertainments at the Haymarket, and each manager heaped personal ridicule on the other. The feud was carried into the pages of the *Daily Advertiser* and Fielding's paper, *The Jacobite's Journal*. Fielding presumably won the prize for scurrility with his trial of one "Samuel Fut" in the *Journal's* weekly "Court of Criticism" on a charge of character assassination. The verdict of the judge was that "you Samuel Fut be p-ssed upon, with Scorn and Contempt, as a low Buffoon; and I do, with the utmost Scorn and Contempt, p-ss upon you accordingly."[4]

Another example of Foote's use of a current situation is his exploitation of the rivalry between two volatile leading ladies at Covent Garden. In January, 1756, when Peg Woffington and George Anne Bellamy played Alexander's two wives in Lee's *The Rival Queens*, they quarreled violently about costumes (Mrs. Bellamy's two new Paris gowns having put Woffington's costume to shame). That summer, Foote dramatized the event as the *Green-Room Squabble or a Battle Royal between the Queen of Babylon and the Daughter of Darius.*[5] Unfortunately, this piece too is lost, with only the title remaining as yet another indication of Foote's use of topical allusion.

These revue-type entertainments were given by Foote for many years. *The London Stage* records performances of *Taste, or The Diversions of the Morning,* as late in Foote's career as the summer season of 1776 at the Haymarket, one of these (July 10) being a command performance.[6] The play had two titles because Foote in the 1758–1759 season had taken part of his comedy *Taste* and altered it for the first act of *The Diversions.*[7] The second act, as it is printed by William Cooke, follows the rehearsal formula: Manly and Free-love are spectators at Mr. Puzzle's playhouse where Puzzle (in imitation of Macklin) is giving lessons to his players.[8] However, the version of act 2 given in 1776 differs from that printed by Cooke. The *dramatis personae* correspond to those in Foote's 1761 revision of *Taste* (also known as *Tradedy a-la-Mode*) in which Manly became a satirical portrait of Charles Churchill in retaliation for Churchill's treatment of Foote in *The Rosciad.*[9] Such revisions indicate that Foote's revues were, in certain cases, also his vehicles for revenge.

To some extent Foote continued this use of improvisation throughout his dramatic career. Often his plays were drastically altered after the first few nights' run, generally in accordance with the audience's reactions, for, as Mary Megie Belden pointed out in the first scholarly study of Foote, notices frequently appeared in the press promising revision of a play which had failed to please.[10] *The Minor,* eventually one of Foote's greatest successes, had a poor initial reception in Dublin,[11] and was revised and expanded before its appearance in London. Other plays so altered include *Taste, The Primitive Puppet Show, The Orators,* and *The Lame Lover.*[12]

II *Foote's Dramatic Criticism*

Samuel Foote's activities as a critic date from the year he became a playwright. In his early days in London, he had two pieces of dramatic criticism published in pamphlet form. The first, *A Treatise on the Passions, So far as they regard the Stage,* is not dated but probably was written in 1747. After some general remarks on the origin of the passions, and a satirical thrust at Garrick for his authorship of the farce, *Miss in her Teens,* Foote tackles the real subject of his essay, criticism of the acting of Garrick, Quin, and Barry. Here, as Macklin had said of Foote's performance as Othello, we can see the scholar in the young man. He has much to say in praise of Garrick's Lear, and his criticism, when he disagrees with Garrick's interpretation, is based on Lear's character as revealed in the text itself. Quin and Barry are compared in the part of Othello, and both condemned, Quin for his monotonous voice and lack of feeling, Barry for being flat and insipid. Both are castigated for their failure to understand the conduct proper to Othello when he appears as a commanding officer. Barry's interpretation (partly because Foote makes allowances for his inexperience) receives more praise than does Quin's—in fact, Quin is dismissed as generally ineffective in tragedy, although an excellent comedian. Barry, however, is cautioned against a too frequent use of tears:

You have, Sir, I doubt not, been often told; that your Expressions of Grief and Tenderness are very becoming, and they told you Truth; but let not this Persuasion draw you into a Prostitution of the Excellence; for, not to mention that your Judgment will suffer in the Eyes of the Discerning, your hackneying the Passion, and applying it indiscriminately, will take from its Weight, and lower its Force, even with the Injudicious: If you cry one Minute for Joy, and another for Sorrow, as in Lord Townly, a Man would be puzzled to know whether you are angry or pleased.[13]

Foote here reveals the conversational tone and the rather biting quality characteristic of his prose. After briefly praising Macklin's Iago, he devotes four pages to a digression reminiscent of Sterne in its facetiousness and flippancy. The treatise as a whole reveals Foote's early interest in the theater, his keen perception of decorum in acting technique, and that characteristic whimsicality which permits him to conclude a sensible discussion with a babble of merry nonsense.

Foote's second piece of dramatic criticism is a sequel to the first. *The Roman and English Comedy Consider'd and Compar'd* (1747) consists of general remarks on comedy and specific criticism of various comic actors. That "A Classic is read only to be admired, a Modern Writer only to be condemned" (8), Foote attributes to the prejudices instilled into the young together with Latin and Greek. He, however, finds the English comedy superior to the

Roman on two counts. The first, which Foote calls "unity of dialogue," is related to his belief that in comedy two types of character are necessary:

The Humourist is a Man, who, from some Extravagance, or Disease of the Mind, is always saying or doing something absurd and ridiculous; but at the same Time is firmly persuaded, that his Actions and Expressions are exactly proper and right. And so absolutely requisite is this last Circumstance, to the Constitution of a Humourist, that a very elegant and judicious Writer, has made it the Mark by which you are to distinguish him; as Ridicule (says he) is the Test of Truth, so is Gravity of Humour.
 · The Man of Humour, on the other Hand, is always joyous and pleasant; the Humourist is his Food; like the Carrion and Crow, they are never asunder; it is to the Labour and Pleasantry of the former, that you are indebted for all the Entertainment you meet with in the latter. (11–12)

Because the humorist must be consistently recognizable, unity of dialogue becomes important. He praises Vanbrugh for the language of his humorous characters. "Each man has a Language peculiar to himself . . ." (14). That this was Foote's practice as well as his theory is made evident by an examination of his own comedies.

Foote is willing to dismiss the unities of time, place, and action on the somewhat quixotic grounds that they are unsuited to the English love of liberty. More important is that unity which he claims has been added by the English, the unity of character, which requires "that your Character be preserved to the End in every Circumstance; and that he neither say, or do, any thing that might as well have been said, or done, by any other Person of the Play" (20). Shakespeare is praised for giving more "elegant, pleasing, and interesting Entertainment" than any man has ever done, while observing consistently only the unity of character.

Foote finds humor, and not wit, the essence of comedy. Humor is the second attribute in which English comedy excels: "no Nation has more Comedies, no Comedies more diversified humorous Characters" (22). As one might expect from his emphasis on humor over wit, Foote's praise of Congreve is qualified: "All his Humourists are well sketch'd, and generally well begun, but ill conducted. The Author, from an Impatience to show his own Wit, throws it into the Mouths of Characters, who are not, in Propriety, entitled to an Atom" (23). Wit must be subservient to character, or it is useless.

Foote concludes his essay with an examination of the merits of the leading comic actors and actresses of the day. His criticism here is more general than was his treatment of the tragic actors. Quin, Mrs. Clive, and Mrs. Pritchard are praised for their success in certain roles, and, predictably, Garrick, the perennial butt of Foote's criticism, receives only limited approbation: "I think Garrick's Rake a sprightly, merry, entertaining Fellow. I can't say I am fond of cultivating an Acquaintance with his Gentlemen. And as to his Fops, either lively or grave, I have them in utter Abhorrence" (45).

Seen against the background of his plays, this early essay on comedy serves as a caveat against critics. It also illustrates Foote's preference for the comedy of humors, his resulting emphasis on character, and his discerning eye for the foibles of actors, all of which later proved to be important aspects of his own revues and comedies. There is, indeed, some question as to whether Foote can be said to have written comedies. His works are usually designated as farce, and the problem of nomenclature, with its related nuances of approval or derogation, must now be considered.

III *Comedy or Farce*

As suggested above, there is some question among the critics as to whether Foote wrote comedy or farce. Part of this problem has to do with the usage of the two terms during the Restoration and eighteenth century. The word "farce" was used pejoratively in the period (Mac Flecknoe "promis'd a play and dwindled to a farce"), and the distinction between farce and comedy was often only one of length, comedies normally consisting of five acts, farces usually of two or three. A play identified as farce on the title page might be called comedy in the prologue. Often one edition of a particular work is labeled comedy, another designated farce. Again, any form of entertainment which served as an afterpiece was frequently referred to as farce.[14] Contemporary writers and critics such as Dryden, Nahum Tate, Bishop Hurd, Dennis, and Wilkes attempted to distinguish between farce and comedy; and although some critical agreement is in evidence, it seems not to have altered the overwhelming inconsistency with which the two terms were commonly applied.

Theatrical usage of the term farce to indicate a genre dates from at least 1661,[15] although Richard Bevis, in his introduction to *Eigh-*

teenth Century Drama: Afterpieces, places the origins of farce much earlier, in the Commonwealth period (1642–1660) when government edicts forbidding dramatic activity were circumvented by the actors: "In these trying times they hit upon the droll (from 'the droll humours of . . .') or farce ('stuffing'): a brief, amusing selection from a larger play, which could be slipped into the programme along with some lawful entertainment, cost little to produce, and lent itself to a quick getaway."[16] The similarity between this practice and the "concert" formula used so successfully by Foote is striking.

Whatever its origins, farce has nearly always been derogated, as being somehow inferior to, as well as different from, comedy. Dryden, in his preface to *An Evening's Love* (1671), argued that comedy was to be distinguished from farce chiefly on the basis of its remaining within the bounds of nature and probability:

Comedy consists, though of low persons, yet of natural actions and characters; I mean such humours, adventures, and designs as are to be found and met with in the world. Farce, on the other side, consists of forced humours and unnatural events. Comedy presents us with the imperfections of human nature. Farce entertains us with what is monstrous and chimerical: the one causes laughter in those who can judge of men and manners, by the lively representation of their folly or corruption; the other produces the same effect in those who can judge of neither, and that only by its extravagances.[17]

Farce, a representation of unnatural characters and improbable events, is clearly to be enjoyed only by the uncultured.

Although Dryden in a sense broke the critical ground, it was Nahum Tate, in his preface to the 1693 edition of *A Duke and No Duke*, who first attempted a defense of farce as a genre. Samuel A. Golden points out that Tate agrees with Dryden that if comedy exceeds the limits of nature and probability it becomes farce, but distinguishes farce from burlesque and buffoonery ". . . because these deviate from 'good sense.' Farce, therefore, was a dramatic form beyond the limits of probability but within the bounds of 'good sense.' . . . It could be satiric through the use of 'drollery, banter, buffoonery, vagaries, and whimsies.' Therefore, according to his understanding, such plays as *The Rehearsal, The Knight of the Burning Pestle* and even *Love and a Bottle* came within its limits. In them were improbability of action, satirical elements, and heightening of mirth. The point that mirth should not be accompanied by a gross shocking of the senses put a limit on farce."[18]

When Tate says that farce can exceed the "limits of nature" within which comedy must be confined, he, like Dryden, is implying that fidelity in representing character is necessary to comedy. As this also is Foote's chief requisite for comedy, it would appear that his plays, so often considered "mere farce" by his detractors, are at least not so by definition. While Dryden implies the artistic worthlessness of farce, however, Tate attempts to remove from the genre the stigma of being a catchall for all forms of slapstick and dramatic coarseness. Farce, for Tate, is in part the province of dramatic satire, which at least suggests that it may serve as a corrective. By citing such plays as *The Rehearsal* as examples of the genre, and with his insistence upon "good sense," Tate presents farce as a respectable form of theatrical activity.

Despite Tate's defence, it is Bishop Hurd's definition of farce, offered in his *Dissertation . . . on the Provinces of the Drama* (1753), which is still in general use. The purpose of comedy is, in his opinion, "the sensation of pleasure arising from a view of the truth of characters, more especially their specific differences" whereas the "sole aim and tendency of farce is to excite laughter."[19] The slightly moralistic bias of Hurd's criticism is evident. Farce can in some measure delight (although the traditional eighteenth-century association of farce with the debased literary taste of a vulgar lower- and middle-class audience makes even this problematical), but it cannot instruct.

Foote of course insisted that his plays were comedies. In fact, by defining farce as "a sort of hodge-podge dressed by a Gothic cook, where the mangled limbs of probability, common-sense, and decency are served up to gratify the voracious cravings of the most depraved appetites,"[20] he effectively denied that the genre had any claim to dramatic respectability. In his dedication to *Taste,* he took issue with the critics, defending his play's right to be considered comedy:

It may be thought presumptuous of me to have dignified so short a Performance with the Name of a Comedy; but when my Reasons why it cannot be called a Farce are considered, the Critics must indulge me with the Use of that Title; at least till they can furnish me with a better. As the Follies and Absurdities of Men are the sole Objects of Comedy, so the Powers of the Imagination (Plot and Incident excepted) are in this Kind of Writing greatly restrained. No unnatural Assemblages, no Creatures of the Fancy, can procure the Protection of the Comic Muse; Men and Things must appear as they are. It is employed either in debasing lofty Subjects, or in raising humble Ones. (vi)

That Foote associated satire with comedy is evident from the foregoing defense, as well as from his remarks in the preface to the same play, where he specifies the objects of his satire. Both preface and dedication illustrate Foote's stress on the the corrective aspect of comedy. Foote's writings on comedy really apply to the Old Comedy of ancient Greece, the slashing topical satires of Aristophanes, but they are also in agreement with Tate's definition of farce, with one important exception—treatment of character, a facet of Foote's drama which has always been a focus for critical attack.

Few writers from the Garrick era to the present have agreed with Foote that his plays were truly comedy. Among other qualities, their mimicry of known individuals was considered farcical. Samuel Johnson's opinion is perhaps representative:

Boswell. "Foote has a great deal of humour?"
Johnson. "Yes, Sir."
Boswell. "He has a singular talent of exhibiting character."
Johnson. "Sir, it is not a talent; it is a vice; it is what others abstain from.
  It is not comedy, which exhibits the character of a species, as that of a
  miser gathered from many misers: it is farce, which exhibits individu-
  als."[21]

Another contemporary assessment of Foote is that of a reviewer in the theatrical section of *The Universal Museum,* who writes that ". . . regular comedies are not what the town expects from Mr. Foote; they call upon him for whim, humour, and novelty."[22]

Yet Foote was unswayed. In the pamphlet warfare which followed his production of *The Minor* (1760), he defended his method of creating character, defining comedy as "an exact representation of the peculiar manners of that people among whom it happens to be performed; a faithful imitation of singular absurdities, particular follies, which are openly produced . . . for the correction of indi-viduals, and as an example to the whole community."[23] Here we arrive at the crux of the problem. Are characters based on mimicry of actual eccentric personages truly comic? Certainly they are among Dryden's "humours, adventures, and designs . . . to be found and met with in the world," and therefore within the realm of comedy.

But there is a form of aesthetic snobbishness operating in most critical assessments of Foote's characters. He claimed they were realistic, because they were imitations of real people: the Johnsonian view was that realism consisted in representations of the general, not mimicry of the particular. If mimicry stops at satire on the person imitated, it is only mimicry, and its vehicle is farce. If, however, it has a wider implication (the victim seen as type), then it is imitation, and the result is comedy. Like photography as compared with painting, Foote's method was not quite artistically respectable. Furthermore, it was often embarrassing, even painful, to those who had posed unwittingly for a portrait by Foote. It must also be conceded that Foote's avowed purpose of correcting individuals and setting an example to the community was not his sole reason for writing. At the very least, he combined this purpose with a keen financial acumen. Chronically in need of money, he knew the drawing power of his impersonations.

Criticism was, however, not all adverse. Laurence Sterne—like Foote a wit, bonvivant, and above all a creator of memorable characters—admired Foote's gift for ridicule.[24] This admiration is not surprising in view of Sterne's idea of character: "If the characters of past ages and men are to be drawn at all, they are to be drawn like themselves, that is, with their excellencies, and with their foibles . . . and it is as much a piece of justice to the world, and to virtue too, to do the one as the other. . . . I would as soon leave out a man's head as his hobby-horse."[25] Foote might well be continuing Sterne's discussion of hobbyhorses in saying that the ability to discern "those little peculiarities in which the specific difference of characters consists, . . . and draw them to a dramatical point; is the work of a genius."[26]

Richard Bevis has recognized that Foote was at least consistent:

Foote has always been criticised for his libellous caricatures and extreme topicality, in disregard of his repeated claims to be writing Old Comedy. . . . [He] insisted that satire remained the quintessential ingredient. He declared himself "a rebel to this universal tyrant," Love, naming his target as "affectation" and his weapon as "ridicule." Seen in this light, "a comedy's being local or temporary is so far from being a moral or critical fault, that it constitutes its chiefest merit," he argued. To sigh about Shakespeare and universality is to refuse the challenge on his own ground—as most of Foote's detractors have done. The fact remains that Foote stated his critical principles and worked by them with evident conviction for twenty years. In theory and in practice he was the Garrick era's staunchest upholder of the oldest western comic tradition.[27]

Bevis' assessment is unusually generous, and it does make Foote sound more the embattled artist and less the theatrical entrepreneur than he actually was. Yet it is largely the bon mots and cutting witticisms for which he was noted (and which his contemporaries gleefully retold) that give us the picture of Foote as an opportunistic and cruel mimic. The plays and critical writings are, as Bevis states, consistent with the practice of Old Comedy.

Perhaps taking into account Foote's own critical opinions in the foregoing discussion of comedy and farce has tended to obscure the already difficult problem of differentiating between the two. It is surely evident, however, that such differentiation was not consistently practised in Foote's day, and that farce was a term used almost exclusively in scorn. It is equally clear that Foote's plays, like Fielding's, are to be considered a legitimate part of the English comic tradition. Bevis styles them "dramatic satires," and considers their literary antecedents to be "Old and Jonsonian Comedy on one hand, and on the other . . . *The Knight of the Burning Pestle* (1607) and *The Rehearsal* (1671), burlesques on the theatrical absurdities of their day."[28] Mention of the latter two plays, cited also by Tate as farces, together with Tate's admission of satiric content into farce, suggests that we have come full circle, that Old Comedy is a form of dramatic satire, which was for Tate an aspect of farce. To conclude that Foote therefore wrote farce, however, is unfairly to join with the majority of eighteenth century writers who use the term "farce" to derogate the works of other authors. Taking into account, therefore, Foote's emphasis on the corrective aspect of his plays, and considering his affinities with Old and Jonsonian comedy and with the tradition of theatrical burlesque, I have in subsequent chapters referred to his plays as comedies, although I concur with Bevis' use of "dramatic satire" as a description of Foote's works. Perhaps "dramatic satire" begs the question, but it does avoid damning the plays without an examination of their literary merits.

CHAPTER 3

Satiric Modes

I *The Knights*

I N April, 1749, Foote's first regular comedy, *The Knights,* opened
at the Haymarket. In the preface, Foote states that the play
features "three principal characters I met with in a summer's ex-
pedition; they are neither vamped from the French farces, nor the
baseless beings of the poet's brain. I have given them in their plain
habit; they wanted no dramatic finishing; nor can I claim any other
merit than grouping them together and throwing them into action."[1]
Sir Penurious Trifle, Sir Gregory Gazette, and his loutish son Tim
(an early prototype of Tony Lumpkin) are indeed originals and, if
Foote is to be believed, are as firmly based on real people as were
his earlier caricatures of actors and other notable personages from
the London scene. However, because Sir Penurious, Sir Gregory,
and Tim were natives of the West of England, very likely Cornwall,
they were not so easily recognized by London audiences, and could
therefore be appreciated solely as comic creations. It is for this
reason, one suspects, that *The Knights* was considered a "regular"
comedy, although it also displays more extensive plot development
than the earlier revues.

Foote acted the part of the hero, Hartop, in the play and, as
Hartop, impersonated both Tim Gazette and Sir Penurious Trifle,
who otherwise does not appear in the play. The plot turns upon
the fact that both Hartop and Tim are suitors of Miss Sukey Trifle,
Sir Penurious' daughter. Hartop's hope is that in winning Sukey he
will be forgiven his debts to her father. Tim, on the other hand,
has a Cornish sweetheart, Molly Pengrouse, and is being pushed
into a marriage arranged by his parents and Sir Penurious. The
comedy arises from the chance meeting of Hartop and the Gazettes
in a country inn near the Trifle estate, and Hartop's subsequent
contrivances, by the use of various disguises, to win his bride. *The*

Knights has in common with Goldsmith's *She Stoops to Conquer*
and Farquhar's *The Beaux' Stratagem* the setting in a country inn,
the young men coming a-wooing, and the combination of disguise
and mistaken identity. Hartop's frank pursuit of Sukey's dowry is
also reminiscent of Archer's realistic assessment of his financial situation in *The Beaux' Stratagem*. Although the love plot in *The
Knights* is undeveloped—Sukey is hurried into marriage with Hartop in the belief that he is Tim—Hartop, like Archer, is presented
as an impoverished gentleman, and therefore an acceptable husband
for the daughter of a wealthy country family, rather than as an
absolutely unscrupulous fortune hunter. The tone of the play carries
the implication that it is Hartop's right, as a clever and sophisticated
member of a superior class, to deceive the Gazettes, along with
Sukey Trifle and her aunt, in order to marry Sukey and her money.

The *London Stage* lists nineteen performances of *The Knights*
between April 3, when it opened, and June 1, Foote's last appearance of the season.[2] The number of performances and the fact that
the last four were benefit nights indicate the popularity of the piece.
What made this first real play so successful? Like the later works,
it is governed not by the presence of a theme or underlying idea,
but by people, by characteristic modes of behavior, mannerisms,
and peculiarities. These Foote created in both language and action.
At a distance of two centuries we cannot know how much Foote's
acting contributed to the success of his play. Only the printed text
remains, and in it we find several vividly eccentric characters who
make their impact even without the advantage of performance.

Foote's method of presenting character, based as it is on the
representation of various "humours," is well illustrated in *The
Knights*. Sir Penurious Trifle, whose Christian name refers to his
"moral character," is further distinguished by his fondness for telling
long-winded and irrelevant stories. Hartop gives his friend and
fellow conspirator Jenkins a portrait of Sir Penurious:

The very abstract of penury! Sir John Cutler, with his transmigrated stock-
ings, was but a type of him. For instance, the barber has the growth of his
and his daughter's head once a year for shaving the knight once a fortnight;
his shoes are made with the leather of a coach of his grandfather's, built
in the year 1; his male servant is footman, groom, carter, coachman, and
tailor; his maid employs her leisure hours in plain-work for the neighbours,
which Sir Penurious takes care, as her labour is for his emolument, shall

be as many as possible, by joining with his daughter in scouring the rooms, making the beds, &c. thus much for his moral character. Then, as to his intellectual, he is a mere carte blanche; the last man he is with must afford him matter for the next he goes to; but a story is his idol, throw him in that and he swallows it; no matter what, raw or roasted, savory or insipid, dow [*sic*] it goes, and up again to the first person he meets; it is upon this basis I found my favour with the knight, having acquired patience enough to hear his stories, and equipped myself with a quantity sufficient to furnish him; his manner is indeed peculiar, and for once or twice entertaining enough. (9–10)

This portrait is dramatized when Hartop impersonates Sir Penurious in order to deceive the Gazettes.

Sir Gregory Gazette has an appetite for "the news" matched only by his credulity. He is most impressed with Hartop's "news" from London of England's treaty with the pope:

We are to yield him up a large tract of the Terra Incognita, together with both the Needles, Scilly Rocks, and the Lizard-point, on condition that the pretender has the government of Laputa, and the bishop of Greenland succeeds to St. Peter's chair; he being, you know, a protestant, when possessed of the pontificals, issues out a bull, commanding all catholics to be of his religion; they, deeming the pope infallible, follow his directions, and then, Sir Gregory, we are all of one mind. (14)

The comic mode here in *The Knights* is to delineate character and humor. In this respect Foote's theory and practice seem to be in accord. In his preface to *The Comic Theatre* (1762), however, Foote was to make a further claim for comedy. He asserted that "the original purpose of comedy was to expose particular follies for the punishment of individuals, and as an example to the whole community."[3] "The great comic essential" is character, "that specific difference in the mind of one man, which renders him ridiculous to the rest of his contemporaries."[4] The major stress in the 1762 essay is on comedy as a corrective agent. "Plot, incident and all the mechanical parts of a play, are to be considered in a secondary light, and as but the mere vehicles of an important medicine."[5] This is essentially a reassertion of the views on character expressed in his early critical pamphlet, *The Roman and English Comedy Consider'd and Compar'd,* although Foote did not in that essay emphasize the corrective function of comedy. It is easy to grant the supremacy of character in Foote's plays; less easy to agree that comedies like *The Knights* were written as examples to the community.

II   *Taste*

After his 1749 season at the Haymarket Foote abruptly left the stage, probably because he had inherited another fortune. *Taste,* written in 1752 as a vehicle for his friend the comedian Jemmy Worsdale, marked his return, though as Simon Trefman, Foote's most recent biographer, points out, he did not act regularly until becoming a member of the Drury Lane company in October, 1753.[6] *The Knights* had been Foote's first real comedy; in *Taste* he continued to develop his powers as an exponent of comic character, satirizing the follies and foibles of the age.

Taste was first performed on January 11, 1752. In the preface to the play Foote acknowledges "the generosity and Humanity of the Managers of Drury-Lane Theatre" (viii), Garrick and Lacy, in giving Worsdale a benefit performance. Garrick also contributed to Worsdale's benefit by writing a prologue which he delivered in the character of Peter Puff, an auctioneer. Worsdale acted to perfection the part Foote had created for him, Lady Pentweazel. On the first night Foote himself suddenly took over the role of Puff (in the play, not the prologue), giving out to the audience that the comedian, Yates, who had been billed for the part was indisposed. The first act was warmly applauded but the second received a mixed response, and *Taste* was performed only four more times before being withdrawn.[7] Foote says in the preface that the subject of the play was "too abstracted and singular" (viii) for the general audience, suggesting that it might have been more suited to the closet.

The object of Foote's satire in *Taste* was the current antiquarian craze. Two scoundrels, Carmine the painter and Puff the auctioneer, have combined to manufacture and sell spurious old masters and relics of antiquity. The painter is bitterly aware of the vanity and the debased taste of those he preys upon, and blames society for the prostitution of his talent: "As matters are now managed, the Art is the last Thing to be regarded. Family Connections, private Recommendations, and an easy genteel Method of Flattering, is to supply the Delicacy of a *Guido,* the colouring of a *Rubens,* and the

Design of a *Raphael*" (1–2). Carmine's protestations, however, are undercut by his unwillingness to share the profits of his artistic frauds with minor accomplices like Varnish and Brush, and by Puff's angry reminder that Carmine began his career in the fine arts by lettering signs in bawdyhouse windows.

Both men are depicted as avaricious predators. When Carmine rails against the folly of the town Puff counters with cheerful cynicism: "Courage, my Boy! never fear! Praise be to Folly and Fashion, there are, in this Town, *Dupes* enough to gratify the Avarice of us all" (3). Puff illustrates the point in act 2 when he and Carmine, disguised as foreign art experts, dupe the "connoisseurs" who visit his auction rooms.

Aristocratic dilettanti, such as Lord Dupe, credulous citizens, represented by Alderman Pentweazel and his wife, Lady Pentweazel, and pretentious aspiring antiquarians like Novice are briefly but effectively satirized. The prevalence of the fashionable mania for antique and foreign art is further emphasized by mention of Squire Felltree, Jack Squander, and Mordecai Lazarus, "the Jew Broker," representatives of the country booby, the young rake, and the world of commerce. Foote probably took the name Pentweazel from the Pentweazles created by the poet Christopher Smart, who was not only a fellow satirist and sometime provider of theatrical entertainments but also a member of the Delaval circle.[8] *Taste* is dedicated to Francis Blake Delaval, Foote's closest friend.

Vanity is the source of Lady Pentweazel's gullibility. Carmine, preparing to paint her portrait, delineates her character in vivid terms: "Lady Pentweazel! ha! ha! Now here's a Proof that Avarice is not the only, or last Passion old Age is subject to—this superannuated Beldame gapes for Flattery, like a Nest of unfledged Crows for Food; and with them, too, gulps down every Thing that's offer'd her—no Matter how coarse; well, she shall be fed; I'll make her my introductory Key to the whole Bench of *Aldermen*" (2).

Lady Pentweazel, who shares many characteristics with Congreve's Lady Wishfort, dominates act 1 of *Taste*. Her general ignorance and her social pretensions are revealed in mispronunciations such as "Lamskips" (landscapes) and "Haspicols" (harpsichords). Imagery related to farming and the breeding of animals suggests the limitations of Lady Pentweazel's mind. She has had twenty children, though one year she "lay fallow. . . . if Breeding amongst Christians was as much encouraged as amongst Dogs and Horses,

we need not be making Laws to let in a Parcel of outlandish Locusts
to eat us all up" (7), she remarks. Again, discussing the education
of Caleb, her youngest son, she refers to the sending of a child to
boarding school in terms associated with readying animals for market. The economics of the process are of prime importance: "Nay,
the Cost is but small; but poor fourteen Pounds a Year for Head,
Back, Books, Bed, and Belly; and they say the Children are all
wonderful Latiners, and come up, lack-a-day, they come up as fat
as Pigs" (10).

Unrealistically vain about her beauty and her voice, Lady Pentweazel engages in a ridiculous, almost grotesque flirtation with Puff.
It is plain, as Carmine remarks, that Puff could become "a matri-
monial Assistant to a rich Alderman." Apparently there is a limit
to Puff's unscrupulousness, for he answers that he would consider
such a position only "if it were a Sine-cure" (13).

Alderman Pentweazel would perhaps welcome some assistance,
though of a kind different from that suggested by Carmine. Cowed
by his domineering wife, the alderman is seldom allowed to express
an opinion, and is frequently reminded of his stupidity and want
of fine manners. At the conclusion of the play, however, it is he
and Caleb, the Pentweazels' loutish son, who unmask Puff. Un-
moved by his wife's admonitions, the Alderman is skeptical about
the auction itself:

Lady. Now, Mr. *Pentweazel*, let us have none of your *Blowbladder* [Street]
    Breeding. Remember you are at the Court end of the Town. This is a
    Quality Auction.

Ald. Where of Course nothing is sold that is useful—I am tutor'd, sweet
    Honey. (22)

Caleb, uncorrupted by the false taste of the town, has sufficient
common sense to see that the piece of cracked china he has acci-
dentally broken was worthless, and to recognize Puff behind his
black wig and German accent.

Tradesmen, who for the most part lived and worked in the City
of London rather than in the more fashionable West End, or
"Town," in eighteenth-century parlance, are referred to in Foote's
play by the conventional derogatory nickname of "cit." Elsewhere

on the stage, they are almost invariably depicted as ignorant and gullible; in *The Country Wife* Wycherley speaks of a "credulous cit." Often the satire is directed at the social blunders and pretensions of tradesmen and merchants who have risen in the world. Foote's Pentweazels, then, conform to an established satirical convention.

Although Puff's disguise as Mynheer Baron de Groningen, "a great Connoisseur in Painting," has been penetrated, he is unshaken. When Carmine, disguised as another foreign expert, Canto, denies ever having known Mynheer Groningen, Puff quickly incriminates his accomplices, and takes the opportunity of humbling Lady Pentweazel by mimicking her pretensions to the beauty of the Medicis, and her flirtatious overtures to him.

The main objects of the satire in act 2, however, are Lord Dupe and Novice. Aspiring to be known as connoisseurs, they possess neither taste nor a true love of art, but are merely following the fashion. Pride forbids their revealing how the "experts" have defrauded them, as Puff realizes: "My noble Lord here the *Dilettanti*, the *Curieu*, the *Precieu* of this Nation, what Infinite Glory will he acquire from this Story, that the *Leo*, the *Mecaenas* [sic], the *Petronius*, notwithstanding his exquisite Taste, has been drawn in to purchase, at an immense Expence, a Cart-load of—Rubbish! (26). Vanity has led the dupes to affect antiquarian interests, and vanity will keep them silent.

Taste mocks the fashionable preference for all things foreign, and for the ancient above the modern in art; but the piece, though amusing, is slight. There is evidence of hasty writing, especially in the inclusion of several characters such as Sir Positive Bubble and Mordecai Lazarus, who enter in act 2 but are given no speaking parts to integrate them into the action. The play is more revue than comedy, and the satire on cits, predators, and antiquarians not especially original.

At the end of the play, fraud is unpunished, though folly is mocked. The chief merit of *Taste* lies in Foote's delineations of Lady Pentweazel, Puff, and Carmine, each of whom is given particularly appropriate dialogue. These three comic portraits are more memorable than the satire on the would-be connoisseurs, which perhaps accounts for Foote's inclusion of only act 1 of *Taste* in the 1758–1759 version of *The Diversions of the Morning*.

III   The Patron

Twelve years later Foote included a satire on connoisseurs in his comedy *The Patron* (1764), which is in many ways the natural sequel to *Taste*. Rust, an elderly antiquarian, has fallen in love with young Juliet Lofty because the tip of her nose resembles that of the Empress Popaea. He has been seen, however, remarks a wit, making love to a statue in Somerset Gardens, "stroaking the marble plaits of her gown," so his affection for Juliet should not be taken seriously. "She's too modern for him by a couple of centuries" (9). Rust's wooing bears this out. His obsession with antiquarian art permeates all his conversation. Juliet, having no desire to be married to a mummy or locked up "to canker and rust in a cabinet" (31), declines to be worshipped as a work of art or a goddess of classical antiquity. The satire is lighthearted, indeed nonsensical, and the character of Rust incorporated into the plot of *The Patron* more successfully than were the connoisseurs in *Taste*, where the sketchy plot development shows that Foote was still working within the conventions of revue.

In *The Patron* Foote also satirizes the lack of taste, discrimination, and common sense displayed by Sir Thomas Lofty, patron of the arts. Cooke says that although some people saw in Lofty an allusion to George Bubb Dodington, Lord Melcombe, the play contained no personal satire.[9] Sir Thomas, afraid to own authorship of his play before it is performed, prevails upon Dick Bever, his niece Juliet's suitor, to acknowledge the piece as his. Sir Thomas's chagrin mounts as his servants and friends return from the playhouse to report the audience's hissing the play off the stage and condemning it as "the vilest stuff they ever had heard" (57), and Bever is finally given Juliet's hand in marriage in return for a promise of silence. Far from being a true patron and judge of the arts, Lofty is characterized as "a rank imposter, the bufo of an illiberal, mercenary tribe; he has neither genius to create, judgment to distinguish, or generosity to reward; his wealth has gain'd him flattery from the indigent and the haughty insolence of his pretence, admiration from the ignorant" (8–9).

Like *Taste*, *The Patron* was not especially successful. It lacked that "drachm of base,"[10] according to Cooke, which the audience expected Foote to provide. That is to say, the satire was too general. In *The Knights*, on the other hand, his first excursion into regular comedy, Foote had relied on humors characters, often based on real eccentrics whose foibles could be mimicked. This formula was to serve him well. Foote's ventures into general satire were to succeed only when liberally seasoned with his "essential comic ingredient," character.

CHAPTER 4

Fashion's Foibles

I The Englishman in Paris

FOOTE enjoyed traveling on the Continent and seized on the traditional contrasts between English and French in fashion and temperament as material for his theater. Playing no favorites, he satirized the affectations of both nations with equal zest. In *The Englishman in Paris* (1753) Foote ridicules the uncouth and ill-mannered Englishman abroad. Another play written to assist friends, it was first performed for Charles Macklin's benefit. Macklin played Buck, his wife Mrs. Subtle, and his daughter Maria Lucinda, the heroine, a part which displayed to advantage her talents as a singer and dancer.[1] Buck, a rough young English blood, has been sent to France by his father, Sir John Buck, who hopes to separate his son from his rowdy sporting companions in England. With his schoolmaster Classic, Buck lodges in the home of Mr. and Mrs. Subtle, who agree to supervise his initiation into Parisian customs.

Subtle, as his name indicates, is a cozener, and his wife little more than a bawd, while the crowd of "honest tradesmen" they have called in to supply Buck with an acceptable wardrobe are former Englishmen who prey on the ignorance of their fellow countrymen visiting Paris. Subtle exacts a high commission from the tradesmen in return for procuring gullible customers. Foote uses one of the tradesmen, a tailor, to satirize the frivolousness of high fashion: "My good fortune commenc'd by a small alteration in a cut of the corner of the sleeve for count Crib; but the addition of a ninth plait in the skirt of marshal Tonerre, was applauded by madam la duchess Rambouillet, and totally establish'd the reputation of your humble servant" (12–13). A society which gives importance to such trivia, Foote implies, deserves to be preyed upon by cozening tradesmen.

Buck is the Englishman in Paris, and the chief vehicle for Foote's satire. He brings with him from England a well-developed prejudice against the French: "The devil a good thing . . . have I seen since I lost sight of Dover; the men are all puppies, mincing and dancing, and chattering, and grinning; the women a parcel of painted dolls: their food's fit for hogs; and as for their language, let them learn it that like it, I'll none on't; no, nor their frippery neither" (11–12). In his aversion to the French language he is like the "pretty gentlemen" described by Classic, "who condescend to use entirely their native language here [and] sputter nothing but bad French in the side–boxes at home" (11). Here, as in many of his plays, Foote depicts English insularity as rooted in ignorance.

The Subtles' attempt to rush Buck into marriage with their ward Lucinda is prevented by the timely arrival of Sir John. His fears that Lucinda is a fortune hunter are dispelled, however, when she is revealed to be the long-lost daughter of his late friend, Sir Gilbert Worthy, and an innocent victim of the Subtles' machinations. Sir John, welcoming Lucinda as a daughter, forbids the marriage until Buck has reformed his manners and morals. As Buck's chief motive for marriage has been a desire to plague his father, this change of plans is no great inconvenience.

Summarizing the plot places undue emphasis on the structure of the play. In practice the plot merely provides a convenient framework for Buck's antics. Even these, while entertaining, are not always in character. When Buck and a French Marquis vie for Lucinda's hand, the Marquis describes the privileges of a Parisian wife: "A perpetual residence in this Paradise of pleasures; to be the object of universal adoration; to say what you please, go where you will, do what you like, form fashions, hate your husband, and let him see it; indulge your gallant, and let t'other know it; run in debt, and oblige the poor devil to pay it" (27–28). Admitting that a woman of spirit can enjoy the same advantages in London, Buck deviates into sense and refuses bluntly such a fashionable marriage, offering alternative benefits: "I have, madam, courage to protect you, good nature to indulge your love, and health enough to make gallants useless, and too good a fortune to render running in debt necessary" (28). Buck is a curious spokesman for these commendable sentiments, for in the play his courage consists in inciting a riot at the theater, while his good nature is closely allied to gullibility.

At the end of the play, Buck has learned little or nothing. Sir

John, however, realizes that "he who transports a profligate son to Paris, by way of mending his manners, only adds the vices and follies of that country to those of his own" (35). In fact, Buck has shown little inclination to adopt the vices and follies of France, and is indeed more foolish and headstrong than profligate. Satirizing the preoccupations of the hearty English squire, Foote neatly illustrates Buck's narrowness. His obsession with hunting is set off by Subtle's obvious impatience and boredom:

Buck. But harkee, Mr. Subtle, I'll out of my tramels, when I hunt with the king.
Mr. Sub. Well! Well!
Buck. I'll on with my jemmys; none of your black bags and jack boots for me.
Mr. Sub. No! No!
Buck. I'll shew them the odds on't! old Silvertail! I will! Hey!
Mr. Sub. Ay! ay!
Buck. Hedge, stake, or stile! over we go! . . .
    Did I tell you what a chace she carry'd me last Christmas Eve? We unkennell'd at—
Mr. Sub. I am busy now; at any other time.
Buck. You'll follow us. I have sent for my hounds and horses.
Mr. Sub. Have you?
Buck. They shall make the tour of Europe with me: and then there's Tom Atkins the huntsman, the two whippers-in, and little Joey the groom comes with them. Dammy, what a strange place they'll think this? But no matter for that; then we shall be company enough of ourselves. (14–15)

Offered a glimpse of Lucinda in conversation with her singing and dancing masters, Buck expresses his delight in the idiom of the hunt: "A brave-spirited girl! She'll take a five-barr'd gate in a fortnight!" (23). It is a question whether he sees Lucinda as a future hunting partner or as a spirited mare. The characterization of Buck as a rowdy young man preoccupied with hunting and buffoonery is skillful, but in trying to fit this youthful eccentric into the mold of even a comic romantic hero, Foote offends against his own first principle of comedy, unity of character.
    As well as affording a showcase for Maria Macklin's talents, the play provided a rich though inconsistent character part for Charles Macklin and later for Foote himself to exploit. Its success seems to have surprised Foote, especially as he considered that Macklin had "by the powers of dullness instantaneously transformed [his English

Buck] into an Irish chairman."[2] Despite its weaknesses, *The En-glishman in Paris* was regularly performed in London until after Foote's death.

II The Englishman Return'd from Paris

The authorship of *The Englishman Return'd from Paris* (1756), a sequel to Buck's adventures in Paris, was for many years the subject of controversy. The playwright Arthur Murphy, one of Foote's friends, apparently planned to write a sequel to Foote's *Englishman in Paris* and to call it *The Englishman Return'd from Paris*, but Foote forestalled him and brought out his own version, anticipating Murphy by two months. Most of Foote's biographers believed that he had in effect plagiarized from Murphy. Murphy's manuscript has recently been found, however, and as Simon Tref-man points out, the two plays have little more than the title in common.[3] Foote's is the better play and by far the wittier satire. In addition, Murphy's version is sentimental, with Buck undergoing a last-minute reformation in order to marry Lucinda.

Foote's version was performed nineteen times during the season, its popularity enhanced to some degree by the furore over its au-thorship. This success, nonetheless, reflects the quality both of the play and of Foote's performance as Buck. The Buck of Foote's *En-glishman Return'd* is much altered from the Buck of *The Englishman in Paris*. His aversion to all things French has now changed to uncritical admiration, and he scorns the English and their customs. He has exchanged the rowdiness of an English blood for the affec-tations of a French fop. Gone too are the decent instincts he once possessed. Only his lack of judgment remains unaltered.

Foote's plot turns on the will of Sir John Buck, who has died, leaving his old friend Crab as executor. Sir John had hoped that Buck and Lucinda would marry, but had bequeathed Lucinda 5000 pounds should she refuse Buck or 20,000 pounds should Buck reject her. Changed in morals as in manners, Buck despises marriage and suggests that Lucinda become his mistress. Amused by her angry refusal, he is unwilling to part with the 20,000 pounds which a formal rejection of her would necessitate. Lucinda, however, de-cides to revenge herself upon Buck and convinces him that she has poisoned his tea (a device Foote may have borrowed from Mrs. Centlivre's *Artifice*).[4] Delighted with Lucinda's spirit, Crab vows to obtain for her the money to which she is entitled. Promising that he will on certain conditions supply the antidote to the poison, Crab forces Buck to renounce all claim to Lucinda, to burn his "tawdry trappings, . . . foreign foppery, . . . washes, paints [and] pomades" (41) and to dismiss his retinue of French servants, whereupon Crab produces his remedy by simply calling forth Lucinda to reveal the deception.

The plot, like that in most of Foote's plays, is essentially a device for incorporating several satirical characterizations, notably that of Buck, with his entourage of French servants, his tutor Macruthen, and his former English friends Tallyhoe and Racket. Incidental hits, however, are scored against lawyers, represented in the play by Mr. Latitat of Staple's Inn. Summoned by Crab to assist him in executing Sir John's will, Latitat lards his sentences with law Latin and legal jargon to the point of unintelligibility. Natural verbosity and a mania for litigation apparently have fitted him for his profession. Crab, desperate to be rid of the lawyer, asks whether "among all your laws . . . are there none to protect a man in his own house," and is answered by statute: "Sir, a man's house is his castellum, his castle; and so tender is the law of any infringement of that sacred right, that any attempt to invade it by force, fraud, or violence, clandestinely, or *vi et armis*, is not only deemed *felonius* but *burglarius*" (9). Latitat is not essential to the plot. After his appearance at the beginning of the play he is not even mentioned again. The caricature of the law and lawyers exists for its own sake, an example of the inspired mockery Foote so seldom resisted.

Crab, the crotchety cynical executor, is comical in his impatience with foppishness and stupidity, but his honesty prevents him from being ridiculous. His apparent misanthropy is a result of the predominance in *The Englishman Return'd* of wholly unadmirable characters. However, not only is Crab's distrust of Lucinda transformed into respect and then into affection, but it is he who recognizes the merits of Lord John, a young nobleman who has returned from France with Buck. Lord John, whose native English common sense and honesty have been enhanced by his travels, is both a foil for Buck and a suitable match for Lucinda, though Foote as usual subordinates sentiment to comedy.

Buck, as the chief comic character, dominates the play. Foote heightened Buck's ridiculousness by having him enter not only in foppish attire, but disheveled and covered with coal dust as a result

of a collision between his carriage and a coal cart. His conversation
is sprinkled with French words, though as Macruthen admits, "he
can caw [call] for aught that he need, but he is na quite maister of
the accent" (11).

The alteration in Buck's personality in *The Englishman Return'd*
reflects the replacement of Classic, his honest schoolmaster in *The
Englishman in Paris*, by Macruthen, an impoverished and opportunistic Scot. Foote's treatment of Macruthen is topical. Crab cor-
rectly assumes before the tutor's arrival that he will be either a
country curate or "some needy highlander, the outcast of his country" (10–11), an allusion to the dispersion of the highlanders after
the Jacobite uprising of 1745. When Macruthen proposes that he
and Crab combine and gain control of Buck's fortune, Crab's caustic
refusal emphasizes the "known honour and integrity" of the Scottish
nation: "One happiness it is, that though national glory can beam
a brightness on particulars, the crimes of individuals can never
reflect a disgrace upon their country" (13). In this rare instance
Foote limited the scope of his satire to one unscrupulous individual,
making comic use of Macruthen's Scottish speech and dress while
carefully exempting honest Scots from his attack.

Buck's French servants also serve as adjuncts to his character.
The virtues of Bearnois, the Swiss porter, consist in "intrepidity in
denying a disagreeable visitor; . . . politeness in introducing a mis-
tress, [and] acuteness in discerning . : . and excluding a dun" (18).
La Loire, a French chef, and La Jonquil, the *valet de chambre*,
complete Buck's retinue. Together the servants epitomize the suave
duplicity, avarice, and foppishness so often attributed to the French.
Buck's mention of "some little fracas" between the English and the
French refers of course to the Seven Years War (1756–1763). Anti-
French satire was therefore particularly timely.

Nor does English folly escape mention. Tallyhoe and Racket,
Buck's former companions who come to view their friend's trans-
mogrification, enter in full cry:

Racket and Tallyhoe without. Hoic a boy, hoic a boy.
Buck. Let me die if I do not believe the Hottentots have brought a whole
    hundred of hounds with them. But they say, forms keep fools at a dis-
    tance. I'll receive 'em *en cérémonie.*
        Enter Racket and Tallyhoe.
Tally. Hey boy, hoix, my little Buck.
Buck. Monsieur le chevalier, votre très humble serviteur.

Tally. Hey.

Buck. Monsieur Racket, je suis charmé de vous voir.

Rack. Anon, what!

Buck. Ne m'entendez vous? Don't you understand French?

Rack. Know French! No, nor you neither, I think, sir Toby, foregad I believe the papistes ha bewitch'd him in foreign parts.

Tally. Bewitch'd and transformed him too. Let me perish, Racket, if I don't think he's like one of the folks we used to read of at school, in Ovid's metamorphis [*sic*]; and that they have turned him into a beast.

Rack. A beast! No, a bird, you fool. Lookee, sir Toby, by the lord Harry, here are his wings.

Tally. Hey! ecod and so they are, ha, ha. I reckon, Racket, he came over with the woodcocks.

Buck. Voilà des véritables Anglois. The rustic rude ruffians! (26–27)

The vivid scene of the two huntsmen, all awkwardness and bluster, harrying their posturing quarry, was the subject of an engraving by Gabriel Smith.[5] Foote, as Buck, wears a long coat with very full skirts and huge cuffs, and carries a large muff. His hair is swept into two "wings" (as Racket calls them) which look rather like asses' ears. Buck's affectations, his *coiffure*, and his rouge are as ludicrous as the coarse buffoonery of Tallyhoe and Racket, and the result a satire on both French and English.

In Crab, Lucinda and Lord John, Foote managed for perhaps the first time to create interesting "good" characters. Crab's sarcasm and initial suspicion of everyone's motives prevent his becoming a pompous wooden figure like Buck's father in *The Englishman in Paris*. Although Lord John is the spokesman for honor and morality, Foote lightens his speech with an occasional pun, and never allows him to finish his declarations of love for Lucinda. Serious or sentimental elements in his character are minimized, therefore, while Lucinda's witty revenge and her unconcealed scorn for Buck set her apart from the stereotype of the virtuous heroine. Foote achieved a kind of balance in *The Englishman Return'd from Paris*, making the good characters sufficiently amusing and clever to hold their own against the rogues and eccentrics whose foibles give comic impetus to the play.

The comedy in both *The Englishman in Paris* and its sequel derives from the central character, Buck, though in the later play he is more consistently drawn, being entirely free of the taint of romantic love. The perennial opposition of English uncouthness and

French sophistication, and of French affectation and English forth-rightness serve as parallel themes of the two plays. There seems to have been no objection to the triteness of the comparison of French and English morals and manners, which recurs in later works. The actor's skill, heightened by a general feeling of animosity toward the French, no doubt contributed much more to the audience's mirth than is evident in the text.

III The Author

In *The Author* (1757), a long-lost father forms the basis of Foote's plot. Young George Cape, an impoverished author, believes his father dead. Unknown to George, Governor Cape has returned from the new world a wealthy man. Wishing to assess his son's character, the Governor becomes part of George's circle.

The reuniting of father and son, however, is subordinate to the antics of two extraordinary characters who dominate the entire play. Mr. and Mrs. Cadwallader, incorporated into the plot as the brother and sister-in-law of Arabella (the girl George hopes to marry) are truly Dickensian in their eccentricity, though they are caricatures of real persons. The Cadwalladers were based on a Mr. and Mrs. Apreece, or Ap-Rice, the uncle and aunt of Foote's lifelong friend, Francis Blake Delaval. Apreece had requested that Foote bring him on the stage, providing a suit of his own clothes for the actor to wear as Cadwallader. As further indication of his singularity, Apreece was convinced that Foote's public exhibition of his peculiarities would bring him the advancement in government circles previously denied him. [6]

Apreece was in fact the incarnation of the Humorist as defined by Foote in *The Roman and English Comedy Consider'd and Compar'd:* ". . . a man, who, from some Extravagance, or Disease of the Mind, is always saying or doing something absurd or ridiculous; but at the same Time is firmly persuaded, that his Actions and Expressions are exactly proper and right" (11). Foote's delight at finding so appropriate a subject is reflected in *The Author* when George Cape's friend Sprightly speaks of Cadwallader: "He may, George, be useful to you in more than one capacity; if your comedy is not crouded, he is a character, I can tell you, that will make no contemptible figure in it" (12). The implication is that Apreece/

Cadwallader's ridiculousness is an inexhaustible source of comic inspiration.

Those mannerisms of speech and appearance which Foote portrayed in Cadwallader were firmly based on Apreece's peculiarities. According to Thomas Davies, the bookseller who was Johnson's friend and Garrick's biographer, Apreece was large, but "encumbered more by his deportment than his corpulence; with a broad, unmeaning stare, and aukward step," which made him look and walk absurdly: "His voice was loud, his manner of speaking boisterous, his words were uttered rapidly and indistinctly; [while] his head was constantly moving to his left shoulder, with his mouth open, as if to recal what he had inadvertently spoken."[7] He was obsessed with his distinguished ancestry. In London, where Apreece was well-known, "people were very jocose about his family pride,"[8] even before Foote wrote *The Author*.

In the play, Sprightly warns George of Cadwallader's eccentricities:

He is a compound of contrarieties; pride and meanness; folly and archness: at the same time that he wou'd take the wall of a prince of the blood, he would not scruple eating a fry'd sausage at the Mews-Gate. There is a minuteness, now and then, in his descriptions; and some whimsical, unaccountable turns in his conversation, that are entertaining enough: but the extravagance and oddity of his manner, and the boast of his birth, compleat his character. (12–13)

One of Cadwallader's recurrent complaints, the truth of which is amply demonstrated, is that he was deprived of an education: "Look'e here, Mr. Cape, I had as pretty natural parts, as fine talents!—but between you and I, I had a damn'd fool of a guardian, an ignorant, illiterate, ecod—he cou'd as soon pay the national debt as write his own name, and so was resolv'd to make his ward no wiser than himself, I think" (17–18). Cadwallader speaks in fits and starts, frequently interjects "hey!" and "ecod!" and returns without fail to his habitual topics: his pedigree, his poor education, and his wife's stupidity.

It is difficult to tell which aspects of Cadwallader's character are pure mimicry of Apreece and which are broad caricature. Family pride and a desire to know literary men are traits common to both, while Mrs. Apreece's dullness probably also had a basis in fact. In October, 1752, Foote had written to John Delaval, "The town is as empty as your Aunt Price's head."[9]

Attempting to establish himself in the Cadwalladers' good graces, George Cape pays court to Becky Cadwallader, whose principal passion, according to Arabella, is "admiration, or rather adoration" (20). Becky, willing to succumb before George has fairly begun the pursuit, is instructed in the rules of the chase:

Cape. . . . . Zooks you are too hasty; the pleasure of this play, like hunting, does not consist in immediately chopping the prey.
Mrs. Cad. No! How then?
Cape. Why first I am to start you, then run you a little in view, then lose you, then unravel all the tricks and doubles you make to escape me.

> You fly o'er hedge and stile,
> I pursue for many a mile,
> You grow tir'd at last and quat
> Then I catch you, and all
> that.

Mrs. Cad. Dear me, there's a deal on't! I shall never be able to hold out long; I had rather be taken in view. (29)

Arabella's timely entrance saves George from being compromised. But Becky, whose instincts are sharper than her wit, senses Arabella's jealousy and eavesdrops while the embarrassed George explains his behavior. This in turn gives rise to an amusing scene where Becky, hovering between anger at George's deception and regret for an opportunity lost, reveals all to Cadwallader, only to have the imbroglio attributed to her own stupidity:

Mrs. Cad. . . . . Why, as I was telling you, first he made love to me, and wanted me to be a hare.
Cad. A hare! hold, ecod, that was whimsical; a hare! hey! oh ecod, that might be because he thought you a little hair-brain'd already; Becky, a damn'd good story. Well, Beck, go on, let's have it out.
Mrs. Cad. No, I won't tell you no more, so I won't.
Cad. Nay, prythee, Beck.
Mrs. Cad. Hold your tongue then: And so there he was going on with his nonsense, and so in come our Bell; and so—
Cad. Hold, hold, Becky, damn your so's; go on, child, but leave out your so's; it's a low—hold, hold, vulgar—but go on.
Mrs. Cad. Why how can I go on, when you stop me every minute? Well,

52   SAMUEL FOOTE

and then our Bell came in and interrupted him, and methought she
looked very frumpish and jealous. . . . And then at first she scolded him
soundly for making love to me; and then he said as how she advised him
to it; and then she said no; and then he said—
Cad. Hold, hold; we shall never understand all these he's and she's; this
may all be very true, Beck, but, hold, hold, hold; as I hope to be saved, thou
art the worst teller of a story—
Mrs. Cad. Well, I have but one word more; and then he said as how I was
a great fool.
Cad. Not much mistaken in that. (*Aside.*) (36–37)

The various mental and verbal eccentricities of husband and wife
are clearly recognizable in this passage, and convey something of
the ludicrous quality of the comedy in *The Author*. Foote's ability
to create appropriate and individualized dialogue for his characters
is evident throughout the play. The existence of models for the
Cadwalladers in no way detracts from this achievement.

Cadwallader is completely unperturbed by his wife's story,
though he feels it ungenerous of George to take advantage of "a
poor ignorant, illiterate; . . . just as if the grand signor, at the head
of his janisaries, was to kick a chimney-sweeper" (33). His anger is
reserved for George's temerity in wishing to marry Arabella, mixing
"the blood of the Cadwalladers with the puddle of a poet." To
enforce his point, the Cadwallader pedigree is produced: "There's
Welch princes, and ambassadors, and kings of Scotland, and members of parliament: Hold, hold, ecod, I no more mind an earl or a
lord in my pedigree, hold, hold, than Kouli Khan wou'd a serjeant
in the train'd bands" (38–39). In addition, the herald's office has
promised "seven yards more of lineals, besides three of collaterals"
for Monday. However, with the revelation of Governor Cape's
identity and George's parentage, Cadwallader sees the prospect of
adding a governor to his pedigree and willingly consents to the
marriage.

As is obvious, it is character rather than plot that gives form to
the play. Indeed, Foote's inclusion of a long-lost father and a young
couple hoping to marry places even more emphasis on Cadwallader's
obsession with his ancestry. Despite this element of personal satire
in *The Author*, it reads well today. Foote's mockery of Apreece is
lighthearted rather than bitter, and though in 1758 Apreece, unable
to persuade Foote or Garrick, successfully appealed to the Lord
Chamberlain to prohibit the play, he seems to have been driven

to this action by the public notoriety *The Author* brought him rather than by distaste for the play itself. Thomas Davies mentions that whenever Mr. Apreece "went to any public place, to the park, the play-house, to an assembly, or a coffee-house,"[10] people stared and pointed at him, and whispered the name "Cadwallader" loud enough to be clearly heard.

The play was a great success, being performed twenty-three times in the first season, 1757. Cadwallader was an excellent vehicle for Foote's talents, and he had fine support from Mrs. Clive as Becky. Foote's exuberant mimicry of Apreece is personal rather than general, but the play also satirizes Grub Street, especially the monopoly of the booksellers. It is not the social satire, however, but the whimsical, absurd humor which is memorable in *The Author*. The device by which Cadwallader is lured away from home is one of those splendidly erratic flights Foote often affords the reader. Sprightly, George's friend, persuades Governor Cape to pose as the interpreter to a fictitious "prince Potowowsky, . . . the Tartarian prince, that's come over ambassador from the Cham of the Calmucks":

Sprightly. His highness has just sent me an invitation to dine with him; now every body that dines with a Tartarian lord, has a right to carry with him what the Latins call'd his Umbra; in their language it is Jablanousky.
Cad. Jablanousky! well?
Spri. Now if you will go in that capacity, I shall be glad of the honour. (25)

Cadwallader, impressed by the titles, goes willingly to dine with the impostors, sits cross-legged on a carpet and endures a vile soup concocted by Sprightly. Like some of the elaborate practical jokes perpetrated by Foote in real life, the episode has the flavor of modern surrealist humor.

In *The Englishman in Paris, The Englishman Return'd from Paris,* and *The Author,* Foote satirized a variety of fashionable excesses. These early plays, primarily vehicles for his special talents as an actor, were increasingly well-constructed, though as always character took precedence over plot. His dialogue in the latter two plays reveals a rapidly maturing talent for employing idiosyncratic language in the creation of character. Nonetheless, up to this time Foote was a mere entertainer, focusing on rather inconsequential subjects for his satire. This situation was to alter in 1760 with the production of *The Minor*, a play which compels recognition of Foote's powers as a social satirist.

CHAPTER 5

The Public Satirist

I The Minor

FOOTE apparently wrote no plays in 1758 and 1759. After the suppression of *The Author* in December, 1758, had put an end to his plans for the London stage he journeyed to Scotland, where well-known actors had not previously visited. In Edinburgh he enjoyed a very profitable season. A second tour to Dublin proved less successful,[1] however, and in the summer of 1760 he returned to the Haymarket with a new comedy.

The Minor (1760), which, as mentioned in chapter 2, had failed in Dublin, became Foote's most famous play. He revised it, and added the introductory scene, the character of Smirk, and the epilogue.[2] The revamped play, now in three acts instead of two, had its London premiere at the Haymarket on June 28, 1760.[3] It had a phenomenal run of thirty-four performances during July and August, and that autumn was produced by Garrick at Drury Lane as a mainpiece, with Foote playing the roles he had originally created, Shift, Mrs. Cole, and Dr. Squintum. It also ran at Covent Garden in competition with Drury Lane.[4]

The Minor attacks religious hypocrisy in general, but George Whitefield, the itinerant Methodist preacher, is singled out for particular notice. Foote declares his subject to be "those itinerant field orators, who, tho' at declared enmity with common sense, have the address to poison the principles, and at the same time pick the pockets of half our industrious fellow subjects" (8). Again, as in *Taste*, Foote employs the rehearsal formula, perhaps because this provided an opportunity to justify his satire.[5] In the introduction, Canker warns the author that in choosing abuses of religion as his subject he is on dangerous ground, but Foote defends himself against the charge of sacrilege:

I look upon it in a different manner. I consider these gentlemen in the
light of public performers, like myself; and whether we exhibit at Tottenham–court, or the Haymarket, our purpose is the same, and the place is
immaterial. . . . Nay, more, I must beg leave to assert, that ridicule is the
only antidote against this pernicious poison. This is a madness that argument
can never cure: and should a little wholesome severity be applied, per-
secution would be the immediate cry; where then can we have recourse,
but to the comic muse? perhaps the archness and severity of her smile may
redress an evil, that the laws cannot reach, or reason reclaim. (8)

Foote's remark that he sees Whitefield as an entertainer, like himself taking in money for a performance, may indicate a bit of professional rivalry on the part of the playwright, especially in view of
the Methodists' condemnation of the theaters. In addition to defending his play, Foote uses the rehearsal format to beg the in-
dulgence of Smart and Canker (and of the real audience) for the
inexperience and timidity of his players.

The plot of the play proper is similar to that of Foote's earlier
work, *The Author*. A young man, Sir George Wealthy, is visited
by his disguised father, Sir William Wealthy, in order that the father
can assess the son's true merits. Critics have long recognized Sheridan's and Goldsmith's indebtedness to Foote for this situation. The
disguised father (or guardian) and son (or ward) are aspects of the
plot in both *The School for Scandal* and *The Vicar of Wakefield*.
In addition, Sheridan's Charles Surface, Little Premium, and Little
Moses correspond to Foote's Sir George Wealthy and his Little
Transfer.[6] The differing views of Sir William and his merchant brother, Richard, on the education of children, are in turn reminiscent
of those of Shadwell's William and Edward Belfond, in *The Squire
of Alsatia;* but Foote, like Shadwell, may have been directly influenced by Terence.

Sir William Wealthy, having allowed his son, Sir George, four
years travel in Germany, has persuaded his brother, Richard, to
inform George that his father is dead. Sir George, as a minor, will
not come into his inheritance for some three months. During this
time, Sir William, disguised as a German baron, plans to bilk his
son of his fortune and thus teach him a lesson in prudence. Sir
William is assisted by a mimic, Samuel Shift, intended by Foote
as a jibe at Tate Wilkinson, who was then giving imitations of Foote
at Covent Garden.

Mrs. Cole, a bawd (a portrait of Mother Douglas, a noted Covent

Garden madam),[7] who calls to offer Sir George "a young country thing," is depicted as a religious convert whose reformation has been effected by the preacher, Mr. Squintum. Her new religion and her old profession are both made obvious in her speech. The state of her soul seems inseparable in Mrs. Cole's mind from the state of her gout, but in any case she has been born again: ". . . in my last illness, I was wished to Mr. Squintum, who stepped in with his saving grace, got me with the new birth, and I became, as you see, regenerate, and another creature" (35). There seems to be a professional mixing of metaphor involved in her rebirth, the carnal mingling absurdly with the spiritual, although her religious terminology is a fairly accurate reflection of Whitefield's Calvinist leanings. The portrait of Mrs. Cole also comes within the well-established tradition of English anti-Puritan satire.

In Mrs. Cole's speeches there is an incongruous mixing of Methodist cant (as Foote chooses to view and reproduce it) with her offers to procure girls for the two men, Sir George and Loader, a sharper employed to assist in Sir William's scheme:

There had I been tossing in a sea of sin without rudder or compass; and had not the good gentleman piloted me into the harbour of grace, I must have struck against the rocks of reprobation, and have been quite swallowed up in the whirlpool of despair. He was the object of my spiritual sprinkling.—But, however, Sir George, if your mind be set upon a young country thing, to-morrow night, I believe, I can furnish you. (33)

To-morrow I hope to suit you—We are to have, at the tabernacle, an occasional hymn, with a thanksgiving sermon for my recovery. After which I shall call at the register office and see what goods my advertisement has brought in. (35)

Since Mrs. Cole's business at the register office has to do with the fact that she has placed an advertisement for servants under seventeen, in order to lure them into prostitution, the conclusion to be drawn is that she can see no incompatibility between her two current interests. The Methodist religion, by extension, is to be considered equally illogical and hypocritical. George Wealthy makes such an allegation after Mrs. Cole has departed with a bottle of his French wine: "How the jade has jumbled together the carnal and the spiritual; with what ease she reconciles her new birth to her old calling!—No wonder these preachers have plenty of proselytes, whilst they have the address so comfortably to blend the hitherto jarring interests of the two worlds" (36).

The "young country thing" provided by Mrs. Cole is really Sir George's cousin Lucy, who has taken refuge with the Methodists after being disowned by her harsh father, Richard Wealthy, for refusing to accept the husband he had chosen for her. Sir George does not know his cousin, but recognizes her innocence and offers her his protection, thus illustrating his own essential goodness. The plot is somewhat abruptly resolved when with Shift's help Sir George forces his father to reveal his identity. Parents and children are reunited, a marriage is planned between Sir George and Lucy, and all ends happily.

Several of the characters in *The Minor* are the stock types of comedy. Sir George Wealthy, the son whose profligacy hides a noble nature, Richard Wealthy, the harsh father, and Lucy, the innocent and injured daughter—all move rather woodenly and pre-dictably through the play. Sir William Wealthy is redeemed from being the typical wise but indulgent father by his ability as a card-sharper and his ridiculous impersonation of the German baron. The memorable characters in the play are, however, Mother Cole and Samuel Shift, both of whom were played by Foote. The gouty, hypocritical old bawd and the fast-talking mimic who illustrates with impersonations his progress from linkboy to player are given nearly all the lines intended to produce laughter.

The Minor was a *tour de force* for Foote. As Shift he imitated in rapid succession Lawyer Capias, a linkboy, a street vendor, Smirk the auctioneer, and, in the epilogue, Dr. Squintum. In addition, Foote played himself in the opening scene and Mrs. Cole through-out the play. These impersonations, each in the appropriate spec-ialized idiom, illustrate Foote's extraordinary versatility and set off in sharp relief the narrowness William Wealthy ascribes in act 1 to his merchant brother: "People who have their attention eternally fixed upon one object, can't help being a little narrow in their notions" (10). These "narrow" people are specialists, or, as Addison called them in *The Spectator*, No. 105, pedants: "A man who has been brought up among books, and is able to talk of nothing else, is a very indifferent companion, and what we call a pedant. But, methinks, we should enlarge the title, and give it everyone that does not know how to think out of his particular profession, and particular way of life." A classic example of such specialization is the nonstop patter of Smirk the auctioneer, who, like his predecessor, Mr. Prig, has "as much to say upon a ribbon, as a Raphael" (53). Foote has caught the narrowness of thought, as well as the characteristic idiom of the types he portrays.

The situations are trite: the young man at the mercy of sharpers and usurers, the innocent girl alone in the world. The plot serves mainly as a device to illustrate character; it is a frame for the portraits of Mrs. Cole, Shift, and Smirk. It is thus in accord with Foote's theory that character is the comic essential and plot is secondary.

Several critics have recognized a pronounced sentimental tendency in *The Minor*, particularly in that part of the plot dealing with Lucy.[8] While the play has some resemblance to sentimental comedy, it is worthwhile remembering that it is not situation alone that makes for sentimentalism. In his valuable study of sentimental drama, Arthur Sherbo points out that it is often the use of repetition and prolongation to emphasize the suffering of the heroine or the repentance of the reformed rake which distinguishes sentimental comedy from romantic comedy or the comedy of manners.[9] Lucy's one major scene is brief, and the pace is fast. George's reunion with his father is skipped over in a sentence. Few of the other characters behave in accordance with the conventions of sentimentalism. Certainly Mrs. Cole and Shift are sufficiently amusing and eccentric to identify them with the laughing rather than the weeping comedy. Several ingredients of the sentimental drama, moreover—the forlorn heroine, the repentant rake, and the harsh father—though present, are largely undeveloped. Although a more comprehensive evaluation of Foote's attitude toward sentimental comedy will be undertaken in chapter 11, the points outlined above may be sufficient to indicate that *The Minor* is not truly in the sentimental tradition.

Many of the characters in *The Minor* are recognizable stock types, and the action is based on stock situations; however, there is incisive social commentary in the play. John Forster, the nineteenth-century critic who did much to rescue Foote's reputation, sees the Wealthys, Sir William and Richard, as elderly men suddenly discovering that they do not understand their children.[10] Times have changed, says Sir William. Even the young apprentice lads who used to spend their Sundays in churchgoing and their holidays taking a bun and beer at Islington or Mile-End are now advanced into the fashionable vices of gaming, duelling, and even bankruptcy. The differing views of the two brothers on the proper way of raising children illustrate practices which were being challenged during the eighteenth century. Richard's banishment of Lucy for her refusal to marry a wealthy man "sordid in his mind, [and] brutal in his manners" (57), is an implied criticism of the arranged marriage. The parallel between Lucy's situation and that of Clarissa Harlowe is evident, although Foote treats superficially the problems Richardson had explored twelve years earlier with acute psychological insight. George Wealthy's education at public school and university, followed by four years of travel in Europe, is scoffed at by his uncle Richard as merely the means of teaching the boy vice and vanity. The custom of sending young men to Europe to broaden their education had been by this time widely criticized, Foote himself having previously devoted two plays, *The Englishman in Paris,* and *The Englishman Returned From Paris,* to satirizing it, and to ridiculing Englishmen who affected French foppery.

Sir George Wealthy is not without wit, as his banter with "the cit," his uncle Richard, reveals in act 2. Foote uses the exchange to satirize both the class consciousness of the aristocracy and the sobersided prudence of the money-conscious middle class. Sir George tells Richard that his career as a merchant has "so stained, polluted, and tainted the whole mass of your blood, [and] thrown such a blot on your escutcheon, as ten regular successions can hardly efface" (44). The irascible uncle is remorselessly goaded until he can no longer reply ironically to Sir George's taunts, and explodes in alliterative fury, "Traduce a trader in a country of commerce!" (47). Richard is outraged, but Sir George, who began in jest, is in turn stung by his uncle's revelation that the family fortune depended on a great-uncle who was a soap-boiler. The satire is two-edged. Richard and Sir George are both, in their way, Addisonian pedants.

Finally, the inclusion in *The Minor* of the pack of predators, the Baron, Transfer, Loader, and Smirk, all of whom prey upon Sir George, is at once a revelation and a condemnation of the machinations of such types in London society.

II *Satire on Religious Hypocrisy*

Still within the field of social commentary, but having broader implications, is the biting satire on religious hypocrisy for which

The Minor is chiefly distinguished. Mrs. Cole's character and speech have been cited previously to indicate the manner in which Foote treats the hypocritical "convert." In addition, the epilogue, spoken by Foote in imitation of Squintum, satirized Whitefield himself. The name Squintum and the description of the preacher as having a "thriving traffic in . . . [his] eye" (65) refer to the fact that Whitefield was cross-eyed. As could be expected, Foote was sharply criticized for making capital of the famous preacher's physical blemish, but he countered with this argument:

If men, with these infirmities, will attempt things which those very infirmities have rendered them incapable of properly executing, it is their own fault if the source that should acquire them compassion degenerates into a fountain of ridicule. My Lord Lanesborough's gout would have hardly found a place in Mr. Pope's page, if it had not hobbled a minuet at court; nor should Dr. Squintum have shown the whites of his eyes at the Haymarket, if he had confined his circumspection to the tap-room of the Bell at Gloucester; or after his admission to the ministry, modestly submitted to the decent duties of a country cure. But if, in despight of art and nature, not content with depreciating every individual of his own order; with a countenance not only inexpressive, but ludicrous; a dialect not only provincial, but barbarous; a deportment not only awkward, but savage; he will produce himself to the whole public, and there deliver doctrines equally heretical and absurd, in a language at once inelegant and ungrammatical, he must expect to have his pretensions to oratory derided, his sincerity suspected, and the truth of his mission denied.[11]

In short, like Swift, Foote claims to have "spared a hump, or crooked nose, / Whose owners set not up for beaux."[12]

The satire in the epilogue is directed at the Methodists' faith in Providence, as exemplified in the story of the widow and the leg of mutton, which in addition ridicules Whitefield's habitual use of such exempla to illustrate his text. The final lines of the epilogue call into question the preacher's use of donations:

> Oh, what you snivel! well, do so no more,
> Drop, to atone, your money at the door,
> And, if I please—I'll give it to the poor. (66)

Keeping in mind that the epilogue of a play was generally a call for applause and continued support, the above lines, given in the person

of a preacher intoning the offertory, reinforce Foote's earlier clas-
sification of Whitefield as a public entertainer. The exemplum of
the widow which begins the epilogue is followed by a sermonizing
application:

> Aye, that might be, ye cry, with those poor souls;
> But we ne'er had a rasher for the coals.
> And d'ye deserve it? How d'ye spend your days?
> In pastimes, prodigality, and plays!
> Let's go see Foote? ah, Foote's a precious limb!
> Old-nick will soon a foot-ball make of him!
> For foremost rows in side-boxes you shove,
> Think you to meet with side-boxes above?
> Where gigling girls, and powder'd fops may sit?
> No, you will all be cramm'd into the pit,
> And croud the house for Satan's benefit. (66)

Foote, having carefully distanced himself by playing Shift imper-
sonating Squintum, here employs theatrical metaphor as religious
exhortation in a passage reminiscent of Clarissa's speech in *The
Rape of the Lock:*

> Why round our coaches crowd the white-gloved beaux,
> Why bows the side-box from its inmost rows?
> How vain are all these glories, all our pains,
> Unless good sense preserve what beauty gains:
> That men may say, when we the front-box grace:
> "Behold the first in virtue as in face!" (V, 13–18)

As in Pope, Foote's theatrical allusions invoke (albeit humorously)
the transitoriness of life, and imply some judgment to come. The
satire on Whitefield and on Methodism, therefore, is in this instance
antienthusiastic but scarcely sacrilegious.

   Forster has suggested that open criticism of Whitefield in fashionable circles was initiated by Foote—Chesterfield and Horace
Walpole having "confined their scorn to their private letters, though
Horace [Walpole], apprehensive of 'a reign of fanatics,' would have
had the Church publicly 'fight and ridicule him.' "[13] Foote's satire
was important, but he was not first in the field. In *Joseph Andrews*
[1742], Fielding had made a notable attack on Whitefield's sermons.
The Minor, however, raised more controversy. The appearance of

the play on stage and in print (also in 1760) provoked violent reactions on the part of Methodism's adherents and opponents. The
lengthy pamphlet warfare which resulted is described in detail by
Belden,[14] and it is sufficient to note here that the controversy of
1760–1771 flared up at intervals, the last outburst occurring when
Foote took *The Minor* to Edinburgh in 1770. Foote did not trouble
to answer the numerous criticisms of his play, confining his defense
to one pamphlet written in 1760, *A Letter from Mr. Foote to the
Reverend Author of the "Remarks," Critical and Christian," on the
Minor.* (His rejoinder to his chief Edinburgh opponent reiterates
the 1760 reply.) Its calm and well-reasoned tone is in contrast to
that found in many of the pamphlets in defense of Whitefield, whose
supporters, understandably incensed by Foote's attack on Methodism, often showed more zeal than logic. Nonetheless, not all the
opposition to *The Minor* can be dismissed so easily. Lady Hun-
tingdon, Whitefield's patroness, not surprisingly attempted to have
the Drury Lane production (autumn, 1760), suppressed; but according to Walpole, so had Thomas Secker, the Archbishop of Canterbury.[15] The Duke of Devonshire, then Lord Chamberlain,
recommended very few alterations in the text, however, perhaps
because the Archbishop would not point out the passages he considered objectionable. When asked about his failure to be specific,
Secker explained that "he had no wish to see an edition of the *Minor*
announced by the author as 'corrected and prepared for the press
by his Grace the Archbishop of Canterbury.' "[16] Foote, as an entrepreneur, no doubt welcomed the free publicity accruing from
controversy occasioned by his play.

The continued popularity of the play suggests the public's approval of Foote's attack on enthusiasm. Whitefield's oratory attracted huge crowds. According to Forster, he had preached to
twelve thousand on Hampton Common, and at Moorfields had de-
nounced the entertainments to a crowd of thirty thousand.[17] Forster
describes the scene at Whitefield's Tabernacle in Tottenham Court
Road:

The wealthy and the wise were there, as well as the ignorant and the poor;
the low and infamous in either sex, jostled against maids of honour and
lords of the bed-chamber; and "among his frequent hearers," says Sir James
Stephen, the most intelligent and admiring of all the witnesses to his fame,
"were Foote and Garrick, who brought away the characteristic and very

just remark that his oratory was never at its full height till he had repeated
a discourse forty times."[18]

Smirk, the auctioneer in *The Minor*, also employs this trick of repetition.

Methodism could have proven a dangerous revolutionary force.
Huge groups of zealous followers, drawn largely from the lower
classes, were united under the leadership of such compelling orators
as Whitefield and John Wesley, who on occasion aroused their
hearers to a state of hysterical frenzy.[19] The revivalist techniques
of the preachers were repugnant to all who advocated reason: enthusiasm was, in the words of Lucy Wealthy, "an infection" (57).

Arthur Murphy, like Foote an actor, manager, and playwright,
reports a conversation on the subject of *The Minor* in which Foote
justified his satire:

[*Murphy*]. But what of your comedy, Mr. Foote? We hear you found it
dangerous to ridicule what is said in church? . . .
[*Foote*]. Why should I find it dangerous to ridicule what is said in a
church, . . . if what is said there deserves ridicule. Is not the crime the
greater if you pick a pocket at church; and is the additional reason why
a man should *not* have done it, to be the only argument why he should
not be punished for doing it? You call profaneness an offence; you will
not have ignorant men idly invoke the name or the attributes of the
Supreme; and may not I ridicule a fanatic whom I think mischievous,
because he is forever polluting that name with blasphemous nonsense,
mixing with the highest the meanest and most trivial things, degrading
Providence to every low and vulgar occasion of life, crying out that he
is buffeted by Satan if only bit by fleas, and, when able to catch them,
triumphing with texts of Scripture over the blessing specially vouch-
safed.[20]

Certainly Foote seems here to hit at what he considers to be a
blasphemous triviality in Whitefield's preaching. The remarks to
Murphy illustrate that, although later ages have recognized the
value of Methodism and the sincerity of Whitefield, Foote apparently believed he was combatting a fanatical charlatan.

The theatergoing public delighted in the satire on Whitefield,
which, it must be stressed, is not as brutal as the controversy it
occasioned would suggest. Mrs. Cole's hypocritical "conversion,"
her bandying about of Puritan-Calvinist terminology, and the por-

trait of Squintum in the epilogue carry the weight of *The Minor*'s attack on "false" religion. Foote performed the play almost 140 times on the London stage alone,[21] and the epilogue, which itself became a specialty,[22] was given repeatedly by Wilkinson and Foote to display their skill at imitation.

The anonymous author of the brief "Life of Samuel Foote," prefixed to the 1809 edition of his *Dramatic Works*, has this to say of Foote's attack on Methodism in *The Minor*: " . . . so happy was the success of this piece, in one respect, that it seemed more effectually to open our eyes, those of the populace especially, in regard to the absurdities of that set of enthusiasts, than all the more serious writings that had ever been published against them" (12). *The Minor* marks Foote's successful emergence as a public satirist. Though personal satire and mimicry were always to be major elements in his plays, a new power to satirize what he considered absurd or dangerous in society was now evident.

CHAPTER 6

Foote's Frolics and Fancies

I The Lyar

THE unevenness of Foote's literary production is nowhere so clearly illustrated as in the three plays which followed *The Minor*. The first, *The Lyar* (1762), is derived from a work by Corneille and can be considered Foote's most regular play; the second, *The Orators* (1762), is, among other things, a parody of Thomas Sheridan's theories of elocution; the third, *The Trial of Samuel Foote for a Libel on Peter Paragraph* (1763), is the playwright's retaliation against George Faulkner, a Dublin printer who had successfully sued Foote for libel.

In the prologue to *The Lyar* Foote claims that as "this polish'd age" prefers the comedy of intrigue to satire or humor he is presenting "a stranger on the stage," a kind of comedy new to him. Naming his source as a play by Lope de Vega, he notes that critics cannot here accuse him of mimicking living men,[1] a probable reference to the controversy over *The Minor*. Again, in *The Orators*, Foote alludes to public taste. He hints at the nature of the play by introducing a character who comes to the theater only to laugh at Foote and his frolics and fancies.

Foote's main source for *The Lyar* was actually Corneille's *Le Menteur*, though he also could have worked from *The Mistaken Beauty* (1685), an anonymous translation of Corneille's play, or from Sir Richard Steele's adaptation of *Le Menteur*, *The Lying Lover* (1703). Belden, however, finds only "a few passages common to Foote and Steele, and not found in Corneille [which] establish an acquaintance"[2] with *The Lying Lover*, and Steele's modern editor, Shirley Strum Kenny, considers that there is no foundation for the tradition that Foote borrowed from Steele: "Examination of *The Lyar* . . . shows no incontrovertible debt; Foote may have worked

from *Le Menteur* or even *The Mistaken Beauty* because there are
no traces of his having borrowed from Steele's many alterations
rather than the translated passages."[3] The debt, if any exists, is
small.

In 1762 Foote published five volumes of French comedies, entitled *The Comic Theatre, Being a Free Translation of all the Best
French Comedies. By Samuel Foote and Others.* Although he probably translated only the first play himself,[4] Foote no doubt knew
Corneille. Corneille's source for *Le Menteur* was *La Verdad Sos-
pechosa,* by Juan Ruiz de Alarcon. As Belden points out, Foote's
reliance on *Le Menteur* is established by his having followed Corneille in wrongly naming Lope de Vega as his source.[5]

The plot and structure of *The Lyar* are borrowed from *Le Menteur.* Determined to taste the pleasures of London, Young Wilding,
a congenital liar, has come up from Oxford without advising his
father. He meets an heiress, Miss Grantham, in the Mall but mis-
takes her name for that of her friend Miss Godfrey. To impress Miss
Grantham, Young Wilding concocts fantastic lies about his career
as a soldier in America. Later, he meets a former university acquaintance, Sir James Elliot, and unaware that the man is his rival,
describes in detail his previous evening's entertainment of Miss
Grantham at a lavish gala on the Thames. This fiction in time
prompts Sir James to challenge him to a duel.

Young Wilding's other lies embroil him further. Old Wilding, a
friend of Miss Grantham's father, has tentatively arranged a match
between his son and Miss Grantham, but Young Wilding, still mistaking the identity of the two ladies, invents a previous secret marriage to a nonexistent Miss Lydia Sybthorp, of Abingdon, Berkshire.
Enamored of Miss Grantham, he directs a *billet-doux* to Miss Godfrey. An amusing scene ensues in which both the ladies keep an
appointment with Young Wilding, though Miss Godfrey remains
hidden. Thinking the lady he woos to be Miss Godfrey, he abuses
his father's choice, Miss Grantham, and reveals that his pretended
marriage was only a device for avoiding the proposed match.

In the denouement Foote departs from both Steele and Corneille.
Miss Grantham engineers a witty revenge on the liar in which Young
Wilding, having confessed to his father the truth about his feigned
marriage, happily agrees to a match with Miss Godfrey, only to
discover when she appears that she is not the lady he has courted.

Finally, Kitty, Miss Grantham's maid, enters and completes his confusion by introducing herself as Mrs. Wilding, the former Lydia Sybthorp. His lies grown into apparent truths, Young Wilding flees, convinced that everyone about him is mad.

Unlike Corneille, Foote does not provide a romantic conclusion to his liar's misfortunes by an improbable transferral of his affections to Miss Godfrey. Sir James Elliot and Miss Grantham are reconciled, but, as Old Wilding says, "to the ladies, . . . no character is so dangerous as that of a lyar" (72); so his plans for his son's future must await proof that the son has reformed. In Steele's play, the hero mistakenly believes he has killed his rival in a duel and spends the last act in mawkish repentance. The play sinks under the load of sentiment with which Steele has burdened it, and as comedy is far inferior to both *Le Menteur* and *The Lyar*.

Having chosen to adapt Corneille, Foote, unlike Steele, added comic touches to the original. His chief addition was the character of Papillion (*sic*)—valet to Young Wilding. In the first scene of *The Lyar*, Papillion seems the typical comic valet. Young Wilding asks him to "discard all distance between us" (6), however, and instruct him in the ways of fashionable London society, whereupon the valet sheds his French accent and reveals himself to be a former Yorkshire schoolmaster. In addition, Foote introduces satire on several favorite topics, the first being Grub Street. After leaving his Yorkshire school Papillion was "recommended to the compiler of the *Monthly Review*," where his career as a critic began: "In obedience to the caprice and commands of my master, I have condemn'd books I never read; and applauded the fidelity of a translation, without understanding one syllable of the original" (9).

Like most publisher's hacks he earned only a pittance, so resolved to find different employment: "I was mightily puzzled to choose. Some would have me turn player, and others methodist preacher; but as I had no money to build me a tabernacle, I did not think it could answer; and as to player,—whatever might happen to me, I was determined not to bring a disgrace upon my family; and so I resolved to turn footman" (10). Foote again juxtaposes player and Methodist preacher, with the implication that they are related occupations.

Papillion's search for a place as a footman is a satire on the English preference for all things French. No success attends his efforts: "Here I was too old, there I was too young; here the last livery was too big, there it was too little; here I was aukward, there I was knowing: Madam disliked me at this house, her ladyship's woman at the next: so that I was as much puzzled to find out a place, as the great Cynic philosopher to discover a man" (11). Finally a Swiss friend advises him to adapt himself to the folly of the town, forget his knowledge of English, and transform himself into a French valet, in which guise all the doors previously closed to him will open of their own accord. Such was the case, and in his years of service as a French valet Papillion has acquired the knowledge of men and affairs he proposes to impart to Young Wilding.

Papillion is a worthy descendant of the witty servant of Roman comedy. His first advice to his young master is that men in London do not appear in their real characters:

Pap. This town is one great comedy, in which not only the principles, but frequently the persons, are feign'd.
Y. Wild. A useful observation.
Pap. Why now, Sir, at the first coffee-house I shall enter you, you will perhaps meet a man, from whose decent sable dress, placid countenance, insinuating behaviour, short sword, with the waiter's civil addition of *A dish of coffee for Dr. Julap,* you would suppose him to be a physician.
Y. Wild. Well?
Pap. Does not know diascordium from diachylon. An absolute French spy, concealed under the shelter of a huge medicinal perriwig. . . . In short, Sir, you will meet with lawyers who practise smuggling, and merchants who trade upon Hounslow-heath, reverend atheists, right honourable sharpers, and Frenchmen from the county of York. (7–8)

The last, of course, is Papillion himself.

Although he is not vital to the plot Papillion's witty remarks on Young Wilding's failing provide wry comedy, more subtle than that in Foote's other plays but perfectly in keeping with the tone of *The Lyar:*

Pap. You will pardon my presumption; but you have, my good master, one little foible that I could wish you to correct.
Y. Wild. What is it?
Pap. And yet it is a pity, too; you do it so very well.
Y. Wild. Prythee be plain.
Pap. You have, Sir, a lively imagination, with a most happy turn for invention . . . now and then in your narratives you are hurried, by a flow of spirits, to border upon the improbable; a little given to the marvellous.

Y. Wild. I understand you: what, I am somewhat subject to lying?

Pap. Oh, pardon me, Sir; I don't say that; no, no: only a little apt to embellish; that's all. To be sure it is a fine gift; that there is no disputing: but men in general are so stupid, so rigorously attach'd to matter of fact—And yet this talent of yours is the very soul and spirit of poetry; and why it should not be the same in prose, I can't for my life determine.

Y. Wild. You would advise me, then, not to be quite so poetical in my prose?

Pap. Why, Sir, if you would descend a little to the grovelling comprehension of the million, I think it would be as well. (13–14)

The ironical tone of Papillion's comments throughout the play serves as a foil to Young Wilding's outrageous lies.

With the exception of Miss Grantham's maid, Kitty,[6] Foote took the other characters from Corneille. They are nicely diversified: Sir James Elliot, a jealous lover, Miss Grantham witty and flirtatious, Miss Godfrey more prudent, and Old Wilding a respectable old gentleman astonished to discover his son's talent for fiction. The wit holds up well, especially where Foote adds the flavor of London life, as in Young Wilding's comment while waiting beneath Miss Godfrey's balcony: "This rendezvous is something in the Spanish taste, imported, I suppose, with the guitar. At present, I presume the custom is confined to the great: but it will descend; and in a couple of months I shall not be surprized to hear an attorney's hackney clerk rousing at midnight a milliner's prentice, with an *Ally, Ally Croker*" (49).

Most of Foote's comedies are built around one or two eccentric characters, inevitably played by the author himself. In *The Lyar* there is no such role, even Papillion's humor being of a dry and subtle kind not particularly well suited to Foote's acting talents. Surprisingly, Foote, who should also have known better than to set up for a beau, chose to play Young Wilding, and critics from Cooke onward have remarked on his physical unsuitability for the part.[7] Perhaps Foote found the role congenial because Young Wilding shares with his creator a certain panache as well as an unconfined talent for invention. As Dr. Johnson once remarked, "Foote is quite impartial, for he tells lies of every body."[8]

The Lyar is not representative of Foote's social satire. Neither content nor characterization are in his usual mode. There are no predators and no eccentrics. Aside from the basic satire on liars there is no real attack on evil or ridiculous elements in society, and as a consequence the comedy lacks Foote's characteristic biting tone. This is not to derogate the charm and whimsical humor of the play. Being unusually free of personal satire and topical allusion, *The Lyar* is as pertinent today as it was in Georgian England.

II The Orators

Regularity of form, which characterized *The Lyar*, is not a feature of Foote's next comedy. *The Orators* is less a play than a series of sketches linked by the most slender of threads. As mentioned previously, act 1 satirizes Thomas Sheridan, who in 1761 and 1762 had given a series of lectures on oratory at the Pewterers' Hall in London.[9] Foote, parodying Sheridan's rather pedantic approach, inserted the following advertisement for a "Course of Comic Lectures on English Oratory" in the *Public Advertiser:*

1. Oratory in general, 2. Its utility demonstrated from its universality, 3. Distinct species of oratory, 4. The present practice peculiar to the English, 5. Necessity of an Academy, 6. The propriety of appointing the Author perpetual professor. The whole to be illustrated in apt instances by a set of pupils long trained to the art, one of which is amazing proof of the force of Genius when properly cultivated.[10]

Obviously Foote exaggerated Sheridan's pedantry. A recent evaluation of Sheridan's book, *Lectures on Elocution* (1762), commends the author's common sense, describing the lectures as "thorough, [and] fairly well written," though "not very profound."[11] Naturally, it was the latter characteristic Foote seized upon.

A variation of the rehearsal formula links the three acts of *The Orators*. As the play opens, Harry Scamper and Will Tirehack, two Oxford dandies on an escapade in London, enter *"booted, with Whips in their Hands, into a Side-Box"* (3). Scamper, announcing that he can hear lectures enough in Oxford, is ready to go off to the alehouse until he sees a favorite whore, Poll Bayliss, in the gallery. He and Tirehack call for the manager and Foote appears in person to reassure them that, though his lecture is serious, they will be entertained as well.

About to commence, Foote is interrupted from the opposite box by Ephraim Suds, a soap-boiler in the city, who has attended the courses given by the "master professor" in Pewterers' Hall, and has now come to learn "speechifying" from Foote. Suds, like many of Foote's hapless cits, owes his ambition to a nagging wife: "Nothing would serve her turn, but that I must be a common-council man this year; for, says Alice, *says she*, it is the *onliest* way to rise in the world" (6). Ephraim and Alice learned much at Pewterers' Hall: "O Lud! it is unknown what knowledge we got; we can read—Oh! we never stop to spell a word now—and then he told us such things about verbs, and nouns, and adverbs, that never entered our heads before, and emphasis, and accent; heaven bless us, I did not think there had been such things in the world" (6). Here Foote mocks both Sheridan's pedantry and the ignorance of his pupils. Ephraim Suds, obtuseness eager to learn, contrasts nicely with Tirehack and Scamper, scholars willing only to jest and dally with whores.

The lecture which comprises most of act 1 is of surpassing dullness. Foote follows his advertised outline and caricatures Sheridan's plodding thoroughness. He employs rhetorical devices with deadening effect. Professor Samuel N. Bogorad, who has done much to foster modern interest in Samuel Foote, has aptly termed Foote's method of caricature *reductio ad absurdum*,[12] and this technique is deftly applied to Sheridan's lectures. Far from decrying their value, Foote praises Sheridan as a public benefactor, suggesting that if an act similar to the military draft bill were passed, and intelligent persons sent at public expense to London, "and there compelled to go through as many courses of the professor's lectures as he shall deem sufficient; . . . a stock of learning [would be] laid in, that will last till time shall be no more" (9). This alone, says Foote, would make England superior to ancient Greece and Rome.

Discussing the utility of oratory, Foote offers a novel example which he attributes with mock-scholarly exactitude to Sir William Temple's *Essay on Poetry*. In Ireland, where the traditional storyteller is still revered, an acquaintance of Sir William's testifies to the power of such bards:

In his wolf-hunting there, when he us'd to be abroad in the mountains three or four days together, and lye very ill at nights, so as he could not well sleep, they would bring one of those tale-tellers, that when he lay down would begin a story of a king, or a giant, a dwarf and a damsel, and continue all night long in such an even tone that you heard him going on whenever you awakened; and he believed nothing any physicians could give had so good and so innocent an effect to make men sleep in any pains or distempers of body or mind. (20)

A visit from one of these storytellers, whom Foote calls "rockers," would be particularly useful at present, he says, when the fluctuation of the currency is causing great concern. Wondering "whether any of these great men are now residing amongst us, under the disguise of chairmen and hackney coachmen," Foote, satirizing the current interest in ancient poetry, offers another alternative. The possibility that it might be "more adviseable to employ those gentlemen who have so lately and successfully rummaged the Highlands of Scotland and Ireland for the remains of Runic poetry in search of the ablest professors; is submitted to the Society for the Encouragement of Arts" (21). Oratory, scholarly investigation, and the new literary cult are all by implication soporific.

Although much of the humor of Foote's lecture must have depended on his mimicry of Sheridan's mannerisms, his seriocomic discussion of the utility of oratory retains a certain appeal. Trefman, in his biography of Foote, terms the satire Swiftian, suggesting that Foote's lecturer "acts the part of a projector"[13] (like those in book 3 of *Gulliver's Travels*). There is a similar wild misapplication of scientific method: Foote alludes to the mathematician Demoivre in his estimate that the actual and potential parliamentarians in a twenty-year period number 20,000, and carefully cites legal precedent for the circumstantial evidence used to compute the number of lawyers in the kingdom. The modern reader may agree with Harry Scamper's "enough of this dull prosing" (22), but Foote evidently held his audience during the lecture. Perhaps his hearers enjoyed the piquancy of seeing the witty actor demonstrate the art of dullness.

After Scamper's interruption, Foote brings on Donald, a young Scot whose amazing progress is to demonstrate the success of his lectures. Speaking in the broadest of Scots accents, Donald displays his oratorical powers, at least until the young dandies' heckling succeeds in utterly confusing him. Foote was not above resorting to obvious racial humor to get an easy laugh.

Act 2 illustrates his pupils' skill in that species of oratory peculiar to the bar. As the entire scene is imaginary, Foote proposes to prosecute an imaginary being, the Cock Lane ghost, which recently had been the subject of much controversy. After the death of Fanny

Lynes, who had lived in Cock Lane, Smithfield, her ghost com-
municated with a young girl, Elizabeth Parsons. By means of mys-
terious scratching and knocking, Fanny was said to have accused
her lover of poisoning her. All London crowded to Cock Lane hoping
to hear the ghostly noises, and eventually, to settle the public furore,
the Lord Mayor of London appointed a committee to determine
whether the ghost existed. Members of the committee, including
Samuel Johnson, Sir John Fielding, the blind magistrate, and the
Reverend John Douglas, later Bishop of Salisbury, carefully examined the evidence, questioning Elizabeth Parsons at the home
of the Reverend Stephen Aldrich, rector of St. John's, Clerkenwell.
They concluded that there was no ghost, and that the girl herself
had made the peculiar noises.[14] Foote's imaginary trial of Fanny
Phantom is at least a parallel to, if not a parody of, this solemn
investigation.

After some rather predictable mockery of legal terminology and
judicial somnolence, the prosecution calls as witness Shadrach Bodkin, a tailor turned Methodist preacher. Like Mrs. Cole in *The
Minor,* Shadrach has "jumbled together the carnal and the spiritual."[15] Foote's anti-Methodist satire in *The Orators* is more direct
than in the earlier play. Bodkin tells how the spirit within him first
spoke:

One day as I was sitting cross-legged on my shop–board, new seating a
cloth pair of breeches of Mr. Alderman Crape's—I felt the spirit within
me, moving upwards and downwards, and this way and that way, and
tumbling and jumbling—at first I thought it was the colic— . . . At last I
heard a voice whispering within me, crying, Shadrach, Shadrach, Shadrach,
cast away the things that belong to thee, thy thimble and sheers, and do
the things that I bid thee. (30–31)

Bodkin describes his teaching of Methodism as not a calling, but
rather "a forcing—a compelling." The verbal ambiguity reflects
Bodkin's endeavors. Moved by the spirit, he "communed with other
men's wives . . . and with widows, and with maidens," and nine
became pregnant. Defense counsel's "Why, this was an active spirit"
(30–31), reinforces the implied connection between sexual excite-
ment and religious enthusiasm.

Witness for the defense called to disprove Bodkin's testimony
that on the first day of January he heard Fanny Phantom's scratch-
ings and knockings, is Peter Paragraph, a one-legged printer. As

Paragraph, Foote caricatured the bizarre mannerisms and misplaced vanity of George Faulkner, the Dublin printer who was Swift's friend and publisher. Faulkner, well known in London, was also a friend of Lord Chesterfield, and it is almost certainly this friendship that is lampooned in Paragraph's "Last week I went to visit a peer, for I know peers, and peers know me" (32).

Foote emphasizes the accuracy of his mimicry by having Terence, an Irishman, call out from an upper box: "Mr. Justice, that little hopping fellow there, that Dublin journal man, is as great a liar as ever was born— . . . what the debble dy'e call him, Pra—Praragraf, but by my shoul, that is none of his name neither, I know the little bastard as well as myself . . ." (35).

Certain the man on stage was the real Dublin printer, Terence is convinced only when Foote admits to the impersonation. Putting the most defamatory remarks about Faulkner into the mouth of a supposed member of the audience is a clever extension of the rehearsal formula. Heckling comments were to be expected from that quarter, and even lines known to be part of a play will differ in their impact from those delivered on the stage. In defense of Foote's insensitivity in mocking a one-legged man, it should be noted that George Faulkner, who on Chesterfield's advice successfully sued Foote for libel, eventually found it worth his while to publish *The Orators*.[16] And after his accident in 1766, when his leg had to be amputated, the indomitable Foote quipped, "Now I shall take off old Faulkner indeed to the life!"[17]

Act 3 satirizes the Robin Hood Society, an amateur debating club which Foote himself had attended.[18] Its members are depicted as tradesmen, and the ensuing debate on the relative merits of porter and Irish whisky is a mixture of excessive formality and incongruous allusions to the debaters' trades. As Foote remarks ironically in his closing address, his pupils have given "glaring proofs of . . . [their] great ability in every species of oratory" (43). Their combination of ignorance and mock-profundity may be, as Trefman suggests, a caricature of parliamentary debate.[19] But since the chairman of the Robin Hood Society was for some time a wealthy baker, Caleb Jeacocke (known as "The Master of the Rolls"),[20] the satire was in all likelihood directed primarily at the debating club itself.

The three acts of *The Orators* are so tenuously connected that the piece falls within the category of revue rather than comedy, which in no way diminishes its value as entertainment. Foote's

satire brings together the various subjects which recently had caught
the attention of the town, lectures on oratory, the investigation of
ghostly manifestations, and amateur debating societies. Appropriately, public interest in these somewhat trivial pursuits is burlesqued in a play which itself makes no pretense of being more than
an amusing diversion.

III The Trial of Samuel Foote

Trefman describes some of the variations which from time to time
were incorporated into *The Orators*.[21] The only one of these to be
printed, however, is *The Trial of Samuel Foote, Esq. for a Libel
on Peter Paragraph,* which was first played with *The Orators* at the
Haymarket on May 11, 1763.[22] As the title indicates, the skit refers
to George Faulkner's libel action. The contest between Counsellor
Demur for the prosecution and Counsellor Quirk acting for (and
acted by) Foote, is conducted in Irish dialect. Many nonsensical
legal arguments are introduced, Demur's appeal to the judge being
representative of the play's broad humor:

My Lord, I am counsel against this Mr. Fot, and a pretty sort of a parson
this Fot is every inch of him (*coughs*)—You may say that—whe—hee—(*a
deep cough*); but I should be glad to know what kind of right now this Fot
has to be any body at all but himself. Indeed, my Lord, I look upon it,
that he may be indicted for forgery—whe-hee-hee (*coughing*)—Every body
knows that it is a forgery to take off a man's hand, and why not as bad as
to take off a man's leg.[23]

The dialogue indicates a personal parody, possibly of Faulkner,
whose distinctive laugh is also a feature of Peter Paragraph's speech
in *The Orators*.

Foote punned freely on the connection between his name and
his mimicry of a one-legged man:

Judge. I agree entirely with my brother Demur, that this Fot is a most
notorious offender, and ought to be taken measure of, and taught how
dangerous a thing it is for him to tread upon other people's toes; and so
as my brother observes, to prevent his being so free with other *people's
legs*—we will lay him by the *heels*.[24]

When both sides for various illogical reasons drop proceedings,

Foote appears to ask Counsellor Quirk (himself) whether he is safe in speaking a few couplets. Cooke explains that Foote, "when retired from the court, slipped off his counsellor's wig and gown, and appeared as himself."[25] Foote's verses were even more specific in their mimicry than the character of Peter Paragraph in *The Orators.* The italicized words, Cooke points out, "were acted in imitation of Faulkner."[26] The piece is worth quoting *in extenso:*

> I will a tale unfold, though strange—yet true;
> The application must be made by you.
> At Athens, once fair Queen of arms and arts,
> There dwelt a citizen of moderate parts;
> *Precise his manner,* and *demure his looks,*
> His mind unletter'd—though he dealt in books:
> *Amorous,* though old; though dull—*loved repartee,*
> And penn'd a paragraph most daintily.
> He aim'd at purity in all he said,
> And never once omitted *eth,* or *ed;*
> In *hath,* and *doth,* was seldom known to fail,
> Himself the hero of each little tale;
> With wits and lords this man was much delighted,
> And once (it hath been said) was near being knighted.
>   One Aristophanes, a wicked wit,
> Who never heeded grace in what he writ,
> Had mark'd the manners of this Grecian sage,
> And thinking him a subject for the stage,
> Had from the lumber cull'd, with curious care,
> His voice—his looks—his gestures, gait and air,
> His affectation, consequence, and mien,
> And boldly launch'd him on the comic scene;
> Loud peals of plaudits through the circles ran,
> All felt the satire—for all knew the man.
> Then Peter—*Petros* was his classic name,
> Fearing the loss of dignity and fame,
> To a grave lawyer in a hurry flies,
> Opens his purse, and begs his best advice.
> The fee secur'd—the lawyer strokes his band—
>   "The case you put I fully understand.
>   "The thing is plain from Cocos's Reports,
>   "For rules of poetry an't rules of courts.
>   "A libel this—I'll make the mummer know it."
> A Grecian constable took up the poet,
> Restrain'd the sallies of his laughing muse,

> Call'd harmless humour—scandalous abuse.
> The bard appeal'd from this severe decree,
> The indulgent public set the pris'ner free;
> *Greece* was to him—what Dublin is to me.[27]

Faulkner won a battle in the Dublin courts but, as Foote claims,
"The indulgent public set the pris'ner free." In reality, the "pris-
oner" had had his trial deferred, ignored the injunction against
performing *The Orators*, then jumped bail and returned to
England.[28]

Foote's address resembles the satirical portraits in verse known
as "characters," which developed from the early seventeenth-cen-
tury English prose imitations of the Theophrastan character. In this
instance, mimicry gave the final touches to the portrait of Faulkner
painted in Foote's couplets. Using Greece as a metaphor for Ireland,
Foote, with a certain lack of humility, draws a parallel between
himself and Aristophanes. The analogy supports his claim to be
writing Old Comedy, and of course reflects his comically pretentious
nickname of "the English Aristophanes".

The Lyar and *The Orators* illustrate Foote's skill in using the
material at hand to create dramatic entertainments. He could plunder Corneille for the ingredients of a regular comedy, and improve
upon his source, or cobble together topical satire and caricatures
of Sheridan and Faulkner in a mélange exactly suited to the public
taste for scandalous amusement.

CHAPTER 7

Portraits of Society

I The Mayor of Garratt

FOOTE'S habit of "taking off" well-known figures and his depiction of social evils in his plays have led naturally to comparisons with his contemporary, William Hogarth, and gained for the playwright the title, "The Hogarth of the Stage." Both Foote and Hogarth caricatured actual persons; both frequently revealed the predatory characteristics of mankind. In certain cases the objects of their satire coincided, as in Hogarth's "Enthusiasm Delineated" (ca. 1761), which, like Foote's *The Minor*, ridicules Methodism, Whitefield, and Mother Douglas. Comparison between the graphic artist and the playwright cannot be pursued at any great length, for while Hogarth's etchings are preserved, Foote's plays as printed lack much of the impact they must have had when Foote or Wilkinson brought the characters alive on stage. One fruitful result of even a superficial comparison, however, is an awareness of the vividly pictorial effect of certain scenes in the plays, especially the "star turns" performed in imitation of the famous or notorious.

The plays to be discussed in this chapter include satire on the *nouveau riche*, on the militia, on corrupt politics, and on arranged marriages and married life, a list which indicates the range of Foote's portraits of society. Each of the works, *The Mayor of Garratt* (1763) and *The Commissary* (1765), was a success in its first season,[1] and in subsequent years was included in Foote's repertoire. These plays, written in the second half of Foote's thirty-year career as actor, manager, and dramatist, can be considered as representative of his mature work.

For a modern reader, *The Mayor of Garratt* is perhaps the easiest of Foote's plays to appreciate. Its satire on corrupt politics, on the fickleness of the mob, and on the trials of married life is still relevant. It is interesting to know that the persons characterized as Matthew

79

Mug, Peter Primmer, and Major Sturgeon were the Duke of New-castle, Thomas Sheridan, and one Justice Lamb,[2] but this knowledge is not essential to an enjoyment of the comic scenes. The play is based on an historical event, a mock election held periodically in the hamlet of Garratt, which lies between Wandsworth and Tooting in Surrey.[3] This fact gives *The Mayor of Garratt* the artistic dis-tinction of being a satire of a burlesque, a burlesque, moreover, in which Foote himself may have participated. In 1761 Foote visited Garratt during the mock election, and, with Wilkes and Garrick, may even have written some of the candidates' addresses.[4] *The Mayor of Garratt* had a long life: over 130 performances by Foote himself,[5] and periodic revivals on the nineteenth-century American and British stages. Percy Fitzgerald, the first twentieth-century biographer of Samuel Foote, reports that the play was "a stock piece" during his school days.[6]

As with many of Foote's plays, the plot of *The Mayor of Garratt* is merely a device for linking certain humorous incidents. The chief landowner of Garratt, Sir Jacob Jollup, entertains his two daughters, their husbands, and an acquaintance, Major Sturgeon, who have assembled to enjoy the election festivities. After campaign speeches outdoors and domestic wrangling within, Jerry Sneak, Sir Jacob's henpecked son-in-law, is chosen mayor, which encourages him to attempt a revolt against his shrewish wife, Molly.

The characters in *The Mayor of Garratt* are among Foote's most memorable creations. Major Sturgeon, the Brentford fishmonger, militiaman, and magistrate, is the vehicle for a comic portrayal of the ineptness of the militia who had been mobilized during the Seven Years War, when French invasion seemed possible. The marchings and countermarchings, culminating in the ill-fated ex-pedition to Hounslow, where Major Molossas received his fatal injury, are pompously related by the self-important Sturgeon:

The Major made a fine disposition: on we march'd, the men all in high spirits, to attack the gibbet where Gardel is hanging; but turning down a narrow lane to the left, as it might be about there, in order to possess a pig's stye, that we might take the gallows in flank, and, at all events, secure a retreat, who should come by but a drove of fat oxen for Smithfield. The drums beat in the front, the dogs bark'd in the rear, the oxen set up a gallop; on they came thundering upon us, broke through our ranks in an instant, and threw the whole corps in confusion. . . . The Major's horse took to his heels; away he scour'd over the heath. That gallant commander stuck both his spurs into the flank, and for some time held by his mane; but in crossing a ditch, the horse threw up his head, gave the Major a dowse in the chops, and plump'd him into a gravel-pit, just by the powder-mills. . . . Whether from the fall or the fright, the Major mov'd off in a month. (10–11)

This rehearsal of the difficulties of maintaining discipline while moving an army through a public place is almost a verbal rendering of Hogarth's "March to Finchly."

The threat of French invasion passed and the Middlesex militia was disbanded. Major Sturgeon, who had gloried in the sound of war without the sense, is reduced to the civilian pastime of mangling quotations: ". . . that is now all over with me. 'Farewell to the plumed steeds and neighing troops,' as the black man says in the play; like the Roman censurer, I shall retire to my Savine [*sic*] field, and there cultivate cabbages" (14). The comic effect produced by having this *miles gloriosus* compare himself to Othello is typical of Foote's technique. Often his characters incongruously quote from or paraphrase Shakespeare, generally *Othello* or *Hamlet*. Though Foote had not met with approval when he tried to act Othello, many of that play's lines obviously stuck in his mind.

The Major's visit to Garratt, ostensibly to help Sir Jacob "in the justicing way," is really an excuse for his flirtation with Sir Jacob's daughter, Molly Sneak. Although Molly is only too willing to retire with Major Sturgeon to the summerhouse, the militiaman is, in Sir Jacob's words, "As harmless in the chamber as the field" (48). His only successful forays are conversational. Despite Belden's assertion that "the assignation is carried to the disgusting lengths of Wycherley or Shadwell,"[7] one feels that the Major's heavy attempts at gallantry are merely parade drill, which is as close as he comes to lovemaking.

Sir Jacob's daughters, Molly Sneak and Jane Bruin, are contrasting types of womanhood. Molly, vain, grasping and ill-natured, responds with almost indecent alacrity to the Major's flattery, meanwhile reviling poor cringing Jerry Sneak for being unworthy of her. Molly's sister Jane, on the other hand, is completely dominated by her husband, the aptly named Mr. Bruin. The two couples are a comic study in marital misery. Jane Bruin is seen but not heard; Jerry Sneak, encouraged by Bruin, for a moment defies his wife before being once more subdued by Molly's tears and temper. Sir Jacob's remonstrances against Bruin's domination of his wife and against Molly's outright contempt for Jerry Sneak represent the middle ground where marriage becomes a human relationship rather than a battle for supremacy. But only Sir Jacob seems human; the two couples whose marital discord is satirized by Foote enlist our sympathy no more than does the bickering of Punch and Judy. This is not to criticize Foote's depiction of character. Indeed, Jerry Sneak, the epitome of the henpecked husband, was greatly applauded by the original audiences for speeches which still retain their flavor. Sneak, a Cockney pinmaker, tells Bruin of his troubles with Molly:

Why, to say the truth, she does now and then hector a little; and, between ourselves, domineers like the devil: O Lord, I lead the life of a dog: why, she allows me but two shillings a week for my pocket. . . . 'tis she that receives and pays all: and then I am forc'd to trot after her to church, with her cardinal, pattens, and prayer-book, for all the world as if I was still a 'prentice. . . . And then at table, I never gets what I loves. . . . No; she always helps me herself to the tough drumsticks of turkies, and the damn'd fat flaps of shoulders of mutton; I don't think I have eat a bit of under-crust since we have been married: you see brother Bruin, I am almost as thin as a lath. (25)

In conversation with Major Sturgeon, however, Jerry has only praise for Molly's beauty:

Major. . . . you must not think of disobliging your lady.
Sneak. I never does: I never contradicts her, not I.
Major. That's right: she is a woman of infinite merit.
Sneak. O, a power: and don't you think she is very pretty withal?
Major. A Venus!
Sneak. Yes, werry like Wenus—Mayhap you have known her some time?
Major. Long.
Sneak. Belike, before she was married?
Major. I did, Master Sneak.
Sneak. Ay, when she was a wirgin. I thought you was an old acquaintance, by your kissing her hand; for we ben't quite so familiar as that—but then, indeed, we han't been married a year.
Major. The meer honey-moon.
Sneak. Ay, ay, I suppose we shall come to it by degrees. (22–23)

Although only Jerry's "werry like Wenus" and the Major's occasional solecism survive in the text, according to a writer in *Bentley's Miscellany* both Sneak and the Major were played with a broad cockney accent:

Jerry Sneak and Major Sturgeon are, in their line, the two most perfect delineations of which the minor British drama can boast. There is no mistaking their identity. They speak the genuine, unadulterated vulgar tongue of the City. Their sentiments are cockney; their meanness and their bluster, their pompous self-conceit and abject humility, are cockney; they are cockney all over from the crown of the head to the sole of the shoe. . . . Nevertheless, while we acknowledge their excellence, we entertain the most intense contempt for them, and feel the strongest possible inclination to fling the Major into a horse-pond, and smother Jerry Sneak in a bason of water-gruel.[8]

The *Miscellany* writer's angry contempt for Sneak and Sturgeon indicates, among other things, that he responds to art as he would to life, and this response is a backhanded tribute to Foote's ability in delineating character. It is also possible that the critic's attitude may not be far from Foote's own view. Treatment of the "cit" in Foote's comedies varies from a sympathetic characterization of the wealthy merchant (Richard Wealthy in *The Minor*, Riscounter in *The Bankrupt*) to a comic exaggeration of the faults commonly attributed to the lower classes, as with Sturgeon and Sneak.

In addition to laughing at the sham battles of the militia and the real ones of married life, Foote in *The Mayor of Garratt* satirizes political corruption and the stupidity of the electorate. Crispin Heel-Tap, in charge of the electors, commands that they be silent and proceed "with all the decency and confusion usual upon these occasions" (29). Confusion does ensue as the fickle mob endorses each candidate in turn, only to repudiate him in favor of the next. Matthew Mug, a caricature of the baby-kissing politician whose promises of preferment are conveniently forgotten, unsuccessfully tries to bribe Crispin, and remarks that "this is the first borough that ever was lost by the returning officer's refusing a bribe" (38). Finally, the mob, thinking to please Sir Jacob, their landlord, elects Jerry Sneak, a man more incapable than any of the candidates.

The tone of the satire in *The Mayor of Garratt* is milder than in most of Foote's other works. The stupidity and pretentiousness of the "cits" are revealed, as is the gullibility of the mob, but no one is hurt. The militia is inefficient, the politicians ridiculous, and even the cuckolding is incomplete. For Jerry, who dances with Crispin Heel-Tap when he finds that Molly and the Major are partners, stupidity itself is a protection against pain. Perhaps Foote is imply-ing that all cits are so protected. Again, within the play, as in reality, this is only a mock election, and a spirit of festivity prevails.

II The Commissary

Such is not the case in *The Commissary* (1765), a three-act comedy satirizing the efforts of Zachary Fungus, a pretentious commissary, to become a gentleman and thereby rise in society. He is preyed upon by his landlady, Mrs. Mechlin, a bawd and marriage broker, a type frequently satirized by Foote (for example, Mrs. Cole in *The Minor,* Mrs. Fleece'em in *The Cozeners,* and Mrs. Match'em in *The Nabob*). Zachary Fungus boasts to his brother Isaac, a sensible tallow-chandler, that he is learning what belongs to gentility, having now been a gentleman "above five years and three quarters" (28). For all his lessons in singing, dancing, oratory, fencing, and riding, Zachary's progress is negligible. Mrs. Mechlin bests him in fencing, and he falls off his wooden horse. His "teachers," all recommended by Mrs. Mechlin, are opportunists and predators.

Zachary Fungus' similarity to M. Jourdain in Molière's *Le Bour-geois Gentilhomme* has been commented on by most critics. W. A. Kinne, analyzing Foote's debt to French comedy, concludes that, although Foote took valuable hints from Molière and from Dan-court's *La Femme d'intrigues,* he combined his borrowings with actuality, and, in the case of Mrs. Mechlin, improved upon his original. [9]

In 1765, when *The Commissary* opened, many such commissar-ies, returned to England after growing wealthy in the Seven Years War, were trying to buy their way into society. Foote's satire strikes at these war profiteers, but is applicable to any dull-witted *nouveau riche.* Zachery Fungus' determination to marry a lady mocks the pedigree-hunting propensity of such types. Mrs. Mechlin, disguis-ing her niece Dolly as Lady Sacharissa Mackirkincroft, "lineally descended from Hercules Alexander Charlemagne Hannibal, Earl of Glendowery, prime minister to king Malcolm the first" (31–32) has arranged that Zachary shall have his lady, and that she, Mrs. Mechlin, will get her percentage. Although the marriage is pre

vented by the disclosure of Dolly's identity, Fungus has signed the
marriage contract and must pay the penalty for defaulting.

Several types of unsuitable marriage are satirized in *The Commissary*. The Widow Loveit, coming to the marriage broker for a
new and preferably young husband before her first month's mourning is over, causes Mrs. Mechlin to remark ironically upon the
prudence of age: "I wonder they don't add a clause to the act to
prevent the old from marrying clandestinely as well as the young.
I am sure there are as many unsuitable matches at this time of life
as the other" (14). Young Loveit's request for an elderly, wealthy
wife results in Mrs. Mechlin's inadvertently matching him with his
own mother, almost making him "guilty of incense" (63), as Zachary
Fungus says. Although Foote exploits the comic possibilities of the
situation, his satire is also directed at marriage brokers like Mrs.
Mechlin, who made a handsome profit from the social climbers and
fortune hunters who utilized their services. Mrs. Mechlin triumphs
over Zachary Fungus because her lawyer has drawn up an unbreak-
able contract. When the commissary calls her a fiend and a harpy,
she replies that the nation should thank her for bilking him:

Is it because I have practised that trade by retail which you carried on in
the gross? What injury do I do the world? I feed on their follies, 'tis true;
and the game, the plunder, is fair; but the fangs of you and your tribe,

> A whole people have felt, and for ages will feel:
> To their candour and justice I make my appeal;
> Tho' a poor humble scourge in a national cause,
> As I trust I deserve, I demand your applause. (64)

Foote was criticized for neglecting poetic justice in allowing Mrs.
Mechlin to emerge triumphant. Otherwise, *The Commissary* met
with favorable reception from the critics, and had a long and successful run.[10]

One rather specialized target for Foote's satire should be mentioned. In act 1, Mrs. Mechlin arranges with Paduasoy, an English
cloth manufacturer, for delivery of "Italian" waistcoats, "Genoa"
velvet, and foreign ribbons, all in truth English goods. She carefully
arranges to publicize her "imported" wares: "Mr. Paduasoy, Lord!
I had liked to have forgot. You must write an anonymous letter to
the Custom-house, and send me some old silks to be seized; I must
treat the town with a bonfire: it will make a fine paragraph for the

papers; and at the same time advertise the public where such things may be had" (25). Because Mrs. Mechlin dupes those who are too ignorant to distinguish between English goods and the imported fabrics which are the fashion, she cynically claims to be aiding domestic manufactures: "Who says now that I am not a friend to my country! I think the Society for the Encouragement of Arts, should vote me a premium. I am sure I am one of the greatest encouragers of our own manufactures" (26).

The only representative of integrity and common sense in *The Commissary* is Isaac Fungus, the tallow-chandler. All the other characters, with the possible exception of Young Loveit, are parasites, predators, or their victims, and the London Foote depicts is harsh, cruel, and amoral.

The impact of Foote's social satire is evident in both plays discussed in this chapter. His general attack upon political corruption and the stupidity of the mob in *The Mayor of Garratt*, while more gentle than most of his satire, is wittily incisive. Furthermore, as Foote merely adapted the annual farcical "election" for stage purposes, the satire is not really designed to correct. In *The Commissary*, a particularly unsympathetic example of the *nouveau riche* has his pretensions and his ignorance mercilessly revealed. The view of society presented in this play is darker and more bitter than in *The Mayor of Garratt*. Mrs. Loveit and Zachary Fungus, overstepping the bounds that reason and nature should impose, become fair prey for Mrs. Mechlin and her confederates. That the avaricious Mrs. Mechlin escapes censure for attempting to acquire part of the commissary's fortune is somehow fitting, in the climate of this play, for it implies that almost everyone is as guilty of fraud and opportunism as she. The similarity in tone to Jonsonian comedy, so often attributed to Foote's works, can be discerned in *The Commissary's* satire on the evils in society.

III *Foote's Portraits*

Garrick and Dr. Johnson were among the many who feared that Foote's talent for caricature would be directed against them. Garrick, of course, had been imitated, along with other leading actors, in Foote's *Diversions*, but in 1769 Foote threatened to caricature the Shakespeare Jubilee and procession organized by Garrick, as

"Drugger's Jubilee"—Abel Drugger in *The Alchemist* being one of Garrick's best comic roles. A mutual friend intervened, and Foote abandoned the idea. However, in view of the strange relationship between Foote and Garrick, which on each side combined admiration and contempt, Foote may well have derived considerable pleasure from worrying Garrick, and may indeed have had no firm plan to produce "Drugger's Jubilee" on the stage. He certainly lost no opportunity to torment Garrick. On the day of the "great dramatic procession" which was intended as one of the high points of the Jubilee, the weather was very cold and wet. Cooke recounts how "Garrick meeting Foote that morning in the public breakfast-room, just in the time of a very heavy shower of rain, exclaimed, with evident chagrin, 'Well, Sam, what do you think of all this?'—'Think of it!' says Foote, 'why, as a *Christian* should do; I think it is *God's revenge against vanity.*' "[11]

Johnson's reaction to Foote's announced intention of caricaturing the doctor (most probably in connection with the Cock Lane Ghost episode in *The Orators*) was to enquire of his host, Thomas Davies the bookseller, " 'what was the common price of an oak stick;' and being answered six-pence, 'Why then, Sir, (said he) give me leave to send your servant to purchase me a shilling one. I'll have a double quantity; for I am told Foote means to *take me off*, as he calls it, and I am determined the fellow shall not do it with impunity.' Davies took care to acquaint Foote of this, which effectually checked the wantonness of the mimick."[12]

Johnson, however, could recognize the corrective aspect of Foote's satire, especially when it was directed at others. In a conversation about Lord Chesterfield's letters to his son, Johnson was told that "Foote had intended to bring on the stage a father who had thus tutored his son, and to shew the son an honest man to everyone else, but practising his father's maxims upon him and cheating him."[13] Johnson approved, but felt that poetical justice would be better served if the son were a complete villain and the father his only victim.

In general, Foote was greatly feared for his ability to recreate noted figures on the stage. His intermittent feuds with theater people like Garrick, Macklin, Thomas Sheridan, and Fielding all stemmed from his mimicry of them. Most people, not as aggressive as Samuel Johnson in expressing their distaste for being publicly ridiculed, were largely powerless to prevent Foote's caricatures.

Only Mr. Apreece and the notorious Duchess of Kingston succeeded in having the Lord Chamberlain forbid plays (*The Author* and *A Trip to Calais*) in which they were portrayed. Despite its often personal nature, Foote's social satire illustrates the fallacies, affectations, and fraudulent practices common in his society, and gives us a collection of mercilessly revealing portraits of the age.

CHAPTER 8

Plays for a One-Legged Actor

I The Devil Upon Two Sticks

THE COMMISSARY was first performed in 1765. The following year, Foote's accident precluded any dramatic production, though in 1767 he composed *An Occasional Prelude* to mark the reopening of the Haymarket Theatre. It was not until 1768 that he again had a new play, *The Devil Upon Two Sticks*, ready for the stage. This was the first of his plays for a one-legged actor. *The Lame Lover* followed in 1770.

The Devil Upon Two Sticks is based on Le Sage's *Diable Boiteux*,[1] though Foote added much topical satire to the basic plot. In the opening scene Sir Thomas Maxwell, the English consul in Madrid, and his sister Margaret discuss the upbringing of his daughter Harriet. Like Richard Wealthy in *The Minor*, Sir Thomas is an authoritarian father; and he blames his sister (a caricature of the historian, Mrs. Catharine Macaulay) for influencing Harriet with her "romantic republican notions" (8). Foote's satire on Mrs. Macaulay is rather mild, probably because, aside from her being a female intellectual, there was little to ridicule. Margaret Maxwell's dialogue fairly bristles with learned references, much to the annoyance of Sir Thomas:

Why the deuce can't you converse like the rest of the world? If you want money to pay off my bills, you move me for further supplies; if I turn away a servant, you condemn me for so often changing my ministry; and because I lock up my daughter, to prevent her eloping with the paltry clerk of a pitiful trader, it is forsooth an invasion of the Bill of Rights, and a mortal stap to the great Charter of Liberty. (5)

The argument on matters of principle is abruptly ended by news

that the "paltry clerk," Harriet's suitor Invoice, has secretly gained
access to Harriet's room.

In Harriet and Invoice Foote parodies the improbably noble lovers in sentimental drama. The episode is reminiscent of George
Colman's *Polly Honeycombe*,[2] also a satire on high-flown sentimentality, though it parodies the novel rather than sentimental drama.
Invoice is no ordinary clerk. Urging Harriet to escape with him
rather than marry a nobleman of her father's choosing, he rather
inappropriately quotes Milton: *"The world is all before us where
to chuse;* and, as we fly from oppression, *Providence our guide"*
(10). The couple's elopement follows. They flee over the rooftop to
the adjacent house of a chemist. To continue the Edenic metaphor
Foote has them discover a Devil imprisoned in a bottle. Released,
the Devil (Foote) transports them by his magical powers to London
where, like the young man in Le Sage's play, they are shown the
sights of the city.

Foote easily accounted for his lameness. In a violent struggle
with a Spanish grandee, the Devil "got lame on this leg, and obtained the nick–name of the Devil Upon Sticks" (16–17). He explains
that he could have assumed a more pleasing form, but being a Devil
of honor, has avoided all disguise and pretense in order to appear
in his own shape.

The framework of the play, with the Devil first explaining the
demonic hierarchy, and then showing London to Harriet and Invoice provides an opportunity for wide-ranging satire. Contractors
and commissaries (in modern terms, war profiteers), lotteries, elec
tions, are all, he says, Lucifer's concern. Belzebub, on the other
hand, a "petulant, waspish, quarrelsome cur," is "the imp of chi-
cane, and protects the rotten part of the law" (8). Uriel and Bel-
phegor are minor devils, the latter having jurisdiction over fraudulent
trade practices, while Uriel is the demon of quacks and mounte-
banks. Foote's Devil proclaims himself to be the real Cupid, not
the laughing cherub of myth and poetry but the god of unsuitable
marriages:

It is true, I do a little business in the amorous way; but my dealings are
of a different kind. . . . My province lies in forming conjunctions absurd
and preposterous: It is I that couple boys and beldames, girls and grey-
beards, together; and when you see a man of fashion lock'd in legitimate
wedlock with the stale leavings of half the fellows in town, or a lady of

fortune setting out for Edinburgh in a post-chaise with her footman, you may always set it down as some of my handywork. (21–22)

This Cupid reigns over the province of sexual desire rather than that of romantic love. The satire is reminiscent of the mockery of inappropriate marriages in *The Commissary*. Foote's attitude toward marriage varies from play to play, though it is inevitably facetious. His plots, as in *The Devil Upon Two Sticks,* often feature a heroine wishing to escape an arranged marriage. On the other hand, lust or greed, as the Devil implies, can lead to equally unsuitable matches. Among Foote's married couples it is difficult to find a pair who live together without bickering. Admittedly, marital bliss is not inherently comic, but the absence of happy marriages in the plays indicates either a somewhat jaundiced view of matrimony, or an inability to portray emotion. Perhaps the two are in fact complementary attributes.

In conversation Foote treated marriage with his customary levity. Despite the satire in his plays against arranged marriages, he personally negotiated a match between his spendthrift friend, Francis Blake Delaval, and a wealthy female acquaintance:

Sir Francis, having *dipped* his estates considerably, turned his thoughts towards matrimony; and as he was a remarkably handsome man, with a fine address and polished manners, he stood fair to establish himself to advantage in this line. Foote happened to be acquainted with Lady Harriet Paulet: a lady with ninety thousand pounds at her disposal, but very plain in her person; and, it is said, equally so in her understanding. He introduced his friend, who soon gained upon her affections, and a day was appointed for the marriage; but a doubt striking Sir Francis, why Foote, whom he knew to be as much in want of money as himself, did not marry her, he put the question to him. "And so I would," said Foote, "but"—"But what, Sir?" said the other, impatiently.—"But that I happened to be already married to my washer-woman."[3]

Cooke explains that "washer-woman" was a familiar name Foote always applied to his wife. He also tells the sequel to the story of Delaval's marriage: "Soon after the death of the above-mentioned lady (who did not long survive her marriage), a mutual acquaintance of the parties meeting Foote, said 'he had just seen Sir Francis dressed in deep mourning, by which he supposed he must have lost some valuable friend'—'Oh! no,' said the other; 'Frank's *only a widower.*' "[4]

In acts 2 and 3 of *The Devil Upon Two Sticks,* Foote attacks abuses in medicine. His parody of physicians is based on an actual dispute between the Fellows and Licentiates of the Royal College of Physicians, in which the Licentiates had used force to gain admittance to a meeting of the comitia of the college.[5] Naturally, Foote treated this wrangling within the profession satirically, but the siege of the College by the Licentiates also gave him the opportunity to introduce characters examplifying the various forms of malpractice and quackery. Foote makes capital out of various approaches to medicine in Drs. Diet, Linctus, and Diachylon (a plaster made from olive oil and lead monoxide), and in old Nat Nightshade; and ridicules national characteristics in Drs. Johnny Macpherson, Sligo, and Osasafras. Dr. Melchisedech Broadbrim the Quaker, and Dr. Habakkuk the Jew are depicted as hypocrites. Both are eager to go to law against the Fellows of the College, though neither will join in the actual siege, the first because he is a pacifist and the latter because he will not break the Sabbath.

Foote played the most amusing of the disputants, Dr. Squib and Dr. Hellebore, both caricatures of noted physicians. Squib, described as recognizable by his shuffle (to account for Foote's lameness) is based on Dr. Richard Brocklesby, friend of Johnson, Burke, and Wilkes.[6] No doubt Brocklesby was grossly misrepresented, but the modern reader can recognize the type: a doctor obsessed with politics, so harassed by the claims of his avocation that he has no time for the practice of medicine or for the dispute within the College. Squib also dabbles in literature:

The nation, the nation . . . engrosses my care. The College! could they but get me a stiptic to stop the bleeding wounds of my—it is there, there, that I feel! . . .

> Could they but cast the water of this land,
> Purge her gross humours, purify her blood,
> And give her back her pristine health again,
> I would applaud them to the very echo
> That should applaud again! (32)

Dr. Squib, frantically dispensing broadsheets and political cartoons to cure Britannia's ills, is ludicrously diminished by the allusion to Macbeth besieged in Dunsinane.

Dr. Hellebore, Foote's third role in the play, is himself besieged with the other Fellows inside the Royal College. In Hellebore Foote lampooned Sir William Browne, a former president of the College. Famous for his pedantry and eccentricity, Sir William took no offense at the caricature and sent Foote his own muff "that nothing need be lacking . . . to so excellent a portrait."[7] In spite of its personal allusions, the satire is timeless. Hellebore demonstrates to a new licentiate, Dr. Last, his research into the causes of disease:

Hellebore. These . . . I attribute to certain animalculae, or piscatory entities, that insinuate themselves thro' the pores into the blood, and in that fluid sport, toss, and tumble about, like mackrel or cod-fish in the great deep: And to convince you that this is not a mere *gratis dictum,* an hypothesis only, I will give you demonstrative proof. Bring hither the microscope!
    Enter a Servant with a microscope.
Dr. Last, regard this receiver. Take a peep.
Last. Where?
Hellebore. There. Those two yellow drops there were drawn from a subject afflicted with the jaundice.—Well, what d'ye see?
Last. Some little creatures like yellow flies, that are hopping and skipping about.
Hellebore. Right. Those yellow flies give the tinge to the skin, and undoubtedly cause the disease: And, now, for the cure! I administer to every patient the two-and-fiftieth part of a scruple of the ovaria or eggs of the spider; these are thrown by the digestive powers into the secretory, there separated from the alimentory, and then precipitated into the circulatory; where finding a proper nidus, or nest, they quit their torpid state, and vivify, and upon vivification, discerning the flies, their natural food, they immediately fall foul of them, extirpate the race out of the blood, and restore the patient to health.
Last. And what becomes of the spiders?
Hellebore. Oh, they die, you know, for want of nutrition. Then I send the patient down to Brighthelmstone; and a couple of dips in the salt-water washes the cobwebs entirely out of the blood. (50–51)

The more esoteric realms of medical research are deliciously parodied in Foote's burlesque of scientific pedantry. The attack on Dr. Hellebore's neglect of his patients is more serious. Immersed in research and administration, he resents the intrusion of hospital duties and prescribes wholesale bleeding and purging for the patients in his wards. The satire is as old as medicine itself, but sufficiently grounded in fact to be valid.

The Dr. Last to whom Hellebore demonstrates his cure for jaundice is portrayed as a cobbler *cum* doctor who has traveled to London to sit for his licentiate. Meeting Harriet, Invoice, and the Devil, he explains his dual occupation:

Last. By trade I am a doctor, and by profession a maker of shoes: I was born to the one, and bred up to the other.
Devil. Born? I don't understand you.
Last. Why, I am a seventh son, and so were my father.
Devil. Oh! a very clear title. And pray, now, in what branch does your skill chiefly lie?
Last. By casting a water, I cures the jaundarse; I taps folks for a tenpenny; and have a choice charm for the agar; and, over and above that, master, I bleeds. (34)

Clearly this is a cobbler who does not, in the words of the adage, stick to his last.

Dr. Last is a master of the malapropism. When his local rector, Dr. Tyth'em, fell "flat in a fit of perplexity," Last was ready with the treatment. "I took out my launcelot, and forthwith opened a large artifice here in one of the juglers: The doctor bled like a pig" (34). The examination of this learned candidate by the Royal College of Physicians is farcical in the extreme. The satire lies in the examination's being so cursory that Last is easily certified as an able physician, lending support to an earlier description of the licentiates as "a parcel of Goths" (26).

Foote's collection of physicians consists mainly of quickly sketched stereotypes. In his treatment of the eccentrics, Squib and Hellebore, the personal satire is overshadowed at least from a distance of two hundred years by the sheer ridiculousness of the characterizations. As the Devil admits when Harriet and Invoice decide that acting is more honorable than the learned professions, the Haymarket, Foote's theater, is "an eccentric, narrow establishment, a mere summer fly!" (51). Appropriately, *The Devil Upon Two Sticks* is also a mere summer fly, good exuberant entertainment. The virtuosity of Foote's invention in such scenes as Hellebore's cure for jaundice, however, elevates the satire to the comic level of Shandean digression.

II The Lame Lover

Having satirized the medical profession in *The Devil Upon Two Sticks*, Foote in 1770 turned his attention to that other perennial target for satire, the law. In his new play, *The Lame Lover*, the plot again hinges on a conflict between father and daughter. Sergeant Circuit is an Addisonian pedant, a man whose specialized interest in the law has driven all other considerations from his mind. Charlotte, his daughter, is one of Foote's more vivacious heroines, partly because she has absorbed enough of Sergeant Circuit's legal jargon to hold her own in debate with her father, and partly because the subject of their argument, his plan to marry her to Sir Luke Limp, is rich in comic overtones.

In Sir Luke, a one-legged bachelor still trying to play the fashionable gallant, Foote again provided himself with a role for a one-legged actor. Far from disguising his disability, he draws attention to it in Charlotte's punning objection to marrying Sir Luke. It would be, she says, "a pretty thing truly, for a girl, at my time of life, to be tied to a man with one foot in the grave" (9).

Sir Luke has been identified as a caricature of John Skrimshire Boothby Clopton, known as Prince Boothby because of his desire to associate with the aristocracy.[8] Foote has Charlotte criticize Luke Limp's "paltry ambition of loving and following titles" (10), and illustrates the point in a farcical scene where Sir Luke receives successive invitations from an alderman, a knight, an earl, and a duke. There is a flurry of servants entering and hastily departing as Sir Luke in turn accepts and breaks each engagement in order to dine with the man of highest rank.

As Charlotte and her brother Jack are aware, Sir Luke's real interest is in their young stepmother. The flavor of Restoration comedy is detectable in the collation scene where Sir Luke, Mrs. Circuit, and her friends Mrs. Simper and Colonel Secret flirt over the sweetmeats and champagne. A fashionable wife, Mrs. Circuit mocks her absent husband. To improve the jest, Sir Luke brings in Sergeant Circuit's peruke on a block. The company is delighted with the likeness:

Mrs. Sim. All his features are there!
Col. The grave cast of his countenance!
Sir Luke. The vacant stare of his eye!
Mrs. Circ. The livid hue of his lips!
Mrs. Sim. The rubies with which his cheeks are enrich'd!
Col. The silent solemnity when he sits on the bench! (41–42)

Mrs. Circuit completes the picture when she clothes the block in

Sergeant Circuit's gown. All this is a preamble to the sham legal contest in which the four engage. Reminded by Sir Luke that the "Sergeant" who seems sulky "is never so happy as when he is hearing a cause" (42), the company runs off to costume themselves for the mock trial. Predictably the real Sergeant Circuit returns home and enters the room in time to take cover under his own gown.

Mrs. Circuit, like Charlotte, obviously has absorbed the elements of law. As counsel for the plaintiff she employs rhetorical skill and specious logic to the nonsensical case of Hobson versus Nobson. Her argument, too lengthy to quote, derives its humor from incremental repetition, parodying the haranguing manner of a lawyer proving a point. Both her address and Sir Luke's verbose rebuttal apparently were based on mimicry of actual lawyers.[9] The scene can be appreciated for itself, however, as a satire on legal quibbling.

Foote increases the comic tension by the obvious but nonetheless effective device of having the Sergeant, hidden beneath his gown, first move the block (head), then sneeze, and finally interrupt Sir Luke's oratory. Much of the humor in *The Lame Lover* arises from Foote's exploitation of similar stock situations. To discover whether Sir Luke, as Charlotte has hinted, has designs on his wife, Sergeant Circuit, knowing the knight's fondness for the bottle, plies him with champagne. The obligatory drunken scene ensues, with Sir Luke confessing that Mrs. Circuit has seduced him, and the two men weeping together.

Details of characterization are also conventional. Mrs. Circuit is depicted as the unfaithful young wife who can brazen out the knight's revelation, while Circuit is the typical deluded old husband, willing to accept the most flimsy of assurances. In his case, the cuckold's traditional gullibility is augmented by Circuit's narrowness, the obsession with law which blinds him to matters of fact.

The complaint that *The Lame Lover* lacked a plot and "leaves all the parties as it found them"[10] is not strictly justified, for at the end of the play Charlotte is free of Sir Luke. Foote cleverly introduces an alternative suitor in young Woodford, heir to several estates, whose attorney, Fairplay, enters in act 2 to ask advice of Sergeant Circuit. Woodford, like his friend Jack Circuit, is studying law in the Temple. As usual, Foote minimizes the romantic aspect of the plot, ingeniously using Jack, who has arranged the meeting between his sister and Woodford, to report the progress of the love affair:

I'll take a peep to see how they go on;—there they are, just in the same posture I left them; she folding her fingers, and he twirling his hat; why they don't even look at each other: was there ever such a couple of—stay, stay, now he opens his mouth—pshaw!—lord! there he shuts it again— hush! I hear somebody coming—no—nothing at all:—mother is safe I am sure,—there is no danger from her—now let us take t'other—[*peeps at the door*] hum!—gadso, matters are mightily mended—there! there! very well—there he lays down the law—now he claps his hand on his heart— vastly pretty, I vow—there he swops with both his knees on the ground— charming!—and squeezes his hat with both hands, like one of the actors— delightful! she wants him to rise and he won't—prodigious moving indeed! (36–37)

In keeping with Foote's earlier declaration that he was "a Rebel to this universal Tyrant,"[11] Love, sentiment is transformed into comedy. The lovers appear on stage together only at the end of the play, when Woodford's prospects of being both lawyer and landowner meet with Sergeant Circuit's tentative approval.

In *The Lame Lover*, as in *The Devil Upon Two Sticks*, traditional subjects for satire are treated within a simple though entirely adequate plot structure. Both plays are lighthearted, and the satire more amusing than harsh. Trefman notes Foote's frequent introduction of topical new material in *The Devil*, pointing out that the play was enormously popular, and brought in a great deal of money, reputedly between three and four thousand pounds in its first season.[12] Neither play can be ranked among Foote's best, although both are rich in theatrical potential, evidence of Foote's characteristic ingenuity in providing himself with vehicles for a one-legged actor.

CHAPTER 9

Money and Society

I The Maid of Bath

AFTER his satires on physicians and lawyers in *The Devil Upon Two Sticks* and *The Lame Lover,* Foote wrote three plays, *The Maid of Bath, The Nabob,* and *The Bankrupt,* which, though sharing no strong thematic link, are in general concerned with the acquisition and abuse of wealth, and with the connection between money and marriage. His interest in these topics was not new. They are touched on in many of his comedies, and reflect the influence of economic factors on the structure of eighteenth-century society.

In 1771 Foote varied his usual London setting, producing *The Maid of Bath.* Like the two previous plays, *The Maid of Bath* has a lame character, Sir Christopher Cripple; but this one, unlike the others, was not played by Foote, who assigned himself the starring role of Flint. Perhaps he originally visualized the Christopher Cripple part as his own, but had recovered (and learned to use his artificial limb) sufficiently to play the more vigorous role. Indeed, the assigning of a lame role to someone else is a rather gallant indication that Foote was himself again.

Although this play, like *The Minor, The Mayor of Garratt,* and *The Commissary,* is a vehicle for social satire, it is based almost entirely on real incidents and people. Kitty Linnet, the heroine, was in reality Elizabeth Linley, later to become Mrs. Richard Brinsley Sheridan. Solomon Flint, the old miser whom her parents urged her to marry, was Sir Walter Long. The other characters, so Belden states,[1] were all recognizable as members of the Bath scene.

Miss Linley, famous for her voice and her beauty, was engaged to marry Long, but the suit was broken off. Foote makes the breaking of the engagement the basis of his plot, in which Major Rackett, a caricature of another of Miss Linley's admirers, bribes and coaxes

Solomon Flint's cronies to predict the dire consequences of the May–December marriage, whereupon Flint, torn between lust and miserliness, propositions Kitty, thinking to enjoy her as a mistress and later cast her off. Miss Linnet, predictably incensed, refuses, and in the ensuing commotion, Flint is warned by Lady Catherine Coldstream that he will have to make reparation for his refusal to honor the marriage contract.

Personal satire dominates the play, with Long held up to ridicule for his meanness and lasciviousness. *The Maid of Bath*, like *The Minor*, also satirizes the arranged marriage. The greed and pride which motivate parents to bestow their daughters in order to enhance their own financial and social positions are personified in Mrs. Linnet, who, like many of her contemporaries, considered the whole duty of children to be obedience in such matters. Lady Catherine Coldstream, Kitty's Scottish protectress, cites her own case in an effort to encourage the girl to accept the financial security of an arranged marriage. Foote does not include in the play a love match for Kitty—she chooses to continue her career as a singer—but he does show how the older generation prizes status and security.

As previously mentioned, Foote caricatures several members of the circle which frequented Bath as the fashionable place for drinking and gaming. Among the most striking portraits are Major Rackett and Sir Christopher Cripple, a gouty old rake, always, like Falstaff, on the brink of reformation. The Major banters Sir Christopher about his proposal to reform:

Well then, my dear Sir Christopher, adieu! But, if we must part, let us part as friends should; not with dry lips, and in anger. Fillup, take care of the knight. (*Fillup fills the glasses.*) Well, faith, my old crony, I can't say but I am heartly [*sic*] sorry to lose you; many a brave batch have we broached in our time. . . . Don't you remember the bout we had at the Tuns, in the days of Plump Jack? I shall never forget! After you had felled poor Falstaff with a pint bumper of burgundy, how you bestrode the prostrate hero, and in his own manner cried, "Crown me, ye spirits that delight in gen'rous wine!" (11)

The Falstaffian allusions evoked by Major Rackett give to Sir Christopher some of the appeal of Shakespeare's fat knight.

In addition to incorporating in the character of Sir Christopher certain of Falstaff's traits, Foote wrote himself into the play. Lady

Catherine Coldstream warns Solomon Flint that he will be shamed
into paying Miss Linnet damages for breach of contract:

L. Cath. Gad's wull, it sha' cum to the proof: You mun ken, gued folk, at
    Edinbrugh, laist winter, I got acquainted with Maister Foote, the play-
    actor: I wull get him to bring the filthy loon on the stage—
Sir Chr. And expose him to the contempt of the world; he richly deserves
    it. (53–54)

This is of course exactly what did occur, and the actual settlement
of the dispute, with Sir Walter Long paying three thousand pounds
to Mr. Linley, and allowing Elizabeth to keep one thousand pounds
in jewels and other presents, is asserted by John Badcock to be a
direct result of Foote's play.[2] Long and Miss Linley were known
as "Flint" and "The Maid of Bath" for many years.[3]

The first night audience, which included Johnson and Goldsmith,
applauded so enthusiastically that one speech had to be repeated.[4]
The *Theatrical Intelligencer* does not specify which speech, but
several passages of sparkling dialogue might well have earned such
applause. One of the best scenes virtually explodes the pastoral
myth, as Flint describes his country home to Miss Linnet:

Flint. Moreover, that you may live and appear like my wife, I fully intend
    to keep you a coach.
Miss Lin. Indeed!
Flint. Yes; and you shall command the horses whenever you please, unless
    during the harvest, and when they are employed in plowing and carting;
    because the main chance must be minded, you know.
Miss Lin. True, true.
Flint. Though I don't think you will be vastly fond of coaching about; for
    why, we are off of the turnpike, and the sloughs are deadly deep about
    we.
Miss Lin. What, you intend to reside in the country?
Flint. Without doubt; for then, you know, Miss, I shall be sure to have
    you all to myself.
Miss Lin. An affectionate motive!—But even in this happy state, where the
    most perfect union prevails, some solitary hours will intrude, and the
    time, now and then, hang heavy on our hands.
Flint. What, in the country, my dear Miss? not a minute: You will find all
    pastime and jollity there; for what with minding the dairy, dunning the
    tenants, preserving and pickling, nursing the children, scolding the ser-
    vants, mending and making, roasting, boiling, and baking, you won't

have a moment to spare; you will be merry and happy as the days they are long.

Miss Lin. I am afraid the days will be hardly long enough to execute so extensive a plan of enjoyment. (30–31)

Even more likely to have won the audience's approval is Miss Linnet's rejection of Flint, who has asked her to give him proof of her love by repairing with him to his lodgings for premarital intercourse:

Flint. Come, Miss! we have not a moment to lose; the coast is clear: Should somebody come, you will put it out of my power to do what I design.

Miss Lin. Power? Hands off, Mr. Flint! Power? I promise you, Sir, you shall never have me in your power!

Flint. Hear, Miss!

Miss Lin. Despicable wretch! From what part of my character could your vanity derive a hope that I would submit to your infamous purpose?

Flint. Don't be in a—

Miss Lin. To put principle out of the question, not a creature that had the least tincture of pride could fall a victim to such a contemptible—

Flint. Why, but, Miss—

Miss Lin. It is true, in compliance with the earnest request of my friends, I had consented to sacrifice my peace to their pleasure: and, though reluctant, would have given you my hand.

Flint. Vastly well!

Miss Lin. What motive, but obedience to them, could I have had in forming an union with you? Did you presume I was struck with your personal merit, or think the sordidness of your mind and manners would tempt me?

Flint. Really, Miss, this is carrying—

Miss Lin. You have wealth, I confess; but where could have been the advantage to me? As a reward for becoming your drudge, I might perhaps have received a scanty subsistence; for I could hardly suppose you would grant the free use of that to your wife, which your meanness had denied to yourself.

Flint. So, so, so! By and bye she will alarm the whole house!

Miss Lin. The whole house? the whole town shall be told! Sure, the greatest misfortune that Poverty brings in its train, is the subjecting us to the insults of wretches like this, who have no other merit than what their riches bestow on them. (50–51)

The Linley–Long dispute was well known, and Foote's audiences constituted a kind of kangaroo court in which sentence was each night passed upon the ex-suitor. The justice of Foote's characterization has been disputed—Long may not have been the monster he appears to be in the plot and the prologue[5]—but after *The Maid of Bath*, no one could doubt the power of Foote as a satirist. This play is perhaps Foote's liveliest and wittiest. The sparkle of the dialogue may indicate that he responded to the romantic and sentimental aspects of Elizabeth Linley's story. Foote, moreover, had now held his patent four years, and the distribution of key parts among several actors reflects the development of a well-trained repertory troupe. Foote, who in less prosperous days had been forced to play many parts, now had a number of comic actors on whose gestures and delivery he could rely, and whose services he could afford.

II The Nabob

Foote's next play, *The Nabob* (1772), also may have been based on real persons. Sir Matthew White, Lord Clive, General Richard Smith, and George Gray, a school friend of Boswell's, have all been suggested as models for the "nabob," Sir Matthew Mite. W. K. Wimsatt, in an article summarizing the evidence for considering each of these as the basis of Foote's Anglo-Indian portrait, concludes that the "nabob" is probably a composite of the latter three men.[6] The play is sufficiently interesting, however, to make the identity of the model for Sir Matthew a matter of secondary importance.

The huge fortunes amassed in India by the nabobs were being spent in England, often in an effort to rival the traditional supremacy of the aristocracy. Some nabobs, like Sir Matthew Mite, engaged in the buying of votes in order to gain a parliamentary seat. The Major and Touchit, waiting to see Sir Matthew, discuss the inflation created by the nabobs:

Mayor. . . . they do a mortal deal of harm in the country: Why, wherever any of them settles, it raises the price of provisions for thirty miles round. People rail at seasons and crops; in my opinion, it is all along with them there folks, that things are so scarce.

Touchit. Why, you talk like a fool! Suppose they have mounted the beef and mutton a trifle; a'n't we obliged to them too for raising the value of boroughs? You should always set one against t'other. (33–34)

Sir John Oldham, an impoverished aristocrat, fears he is in danger of losing his parliamentary seat, as Sir Matthew's money will have more influence on the electors than will his own record as a conscientious representative and kindly landlord. In addition, Mite is in a position to have Sir John imprisoned and all his property seized if Oldham will not consent to his daughter Sophy's marriage to the nabob. Foote's satirical portrayal of the treatment accorded visitors by Sir Matthew and by his servant, Janus, is perhaps applicable to many nabobs, "new gentlemen, who," in Thomas Oldham's words, "from the caprice of fortune, and a strange chain of events, have acquired immoderate wealth, and rose to uncontroled power abroad, find it difficult to descend from their dignity, and admit of any equal at home" (18). Sir Matthew's "dignity" is such that he even refuses to recognize an old school friend. However, Foote includes in the play a qualification of his satire on the corrupt nabob. Thomas Oldham, Sir John's merchant brother, speaks of the nabobs, warning against imputing to others the unprincipled actions of a Sir Matthew: " . . . there are men from the Indies, and many too, with whom I have the honour to live, who dispense nobly and with hospitality here, what they have acquired with honour and credit elsewhere; and, at the same time they have increased the dominions and wealth, have added virtues too to their country" (14–15).

Foote also satirizes colonialism in the play. Explaining the source of the nabobs' wealth, Touchit illustrates how settlements and possessions abroad are exploited:

Why, here are a body of merchants that beg to be admitted as friends, and take possession of a small spot in a country, and carry on a beneficial commerce with the inoffensive and innocent people, to which they kindly give their consent. . . . Upon which . . . we cunningly encroach, and fortify by little and by little, till at length, we growing too strong for the natives, we turn them out of their lands, and take possession of their money and jewels. (34)

Touchit's last sentence describes equally well Sir Matthew's proposed treatment of the Oldhams. In this example of colonial principles applied at home, Foote goes a step beyond satire of the *nouveau riche* as it usually is done.

Another facet of Foote's social commentary is directed at the attitude of the aristocracy toward the rising middle class. Lady Oldham, Sir John's hot-tempered wife, feels that merchants like Thomas Oldham, who "have narrowed their notions with com-

merce," are incapable of the "delicacy . . . [and] elevation of sentiment" (8) necessary to the handling of the Oldhams' financial
problems. Lady Oldham's snobbish attitude, which has prevented
any declaration of love between her daughter Sophy and Young
Thomas Oldham, is changed by the end of the play, when her
merchant brother-in-law forestalls Sir Matthew Mite's planned ruin
of Sir John's fortune. English integrity and experience in commerce
triumph over the unscrupulous dealings of the wealthy nabob.

The denouement is somewhat sentimental. Thomas Oldham prevents his brother's financial ruin, and the engagement of the cousins,
Young Thomas and Sophy, receives parental blessing. This tendency
toward sentimentality in the conclusion is more than counterbal-
anced, however, by the play's revelation of the political and financial
machinations of a powerful new group in English society. Belden
points out that Foote's satire extends far beyond his attack on nabobs: "Though Foote satirizes the nabobs in England, he makes it
clear that their venality could thrive there only because the soil was
adapted to it. Like Molière's Jourdain, like his own Buck and Zach
Fungus, Foote's nabob is at the mercy of those who would teach
him how to behave in society; in his shady amours he is swindled
by one worse than himself, the infamous Mrs. Match-em; in his
political ambitions, he is lured by the corruptibility of constituen-
cies."[7]

The Society of Antiquaries is also an object of Foote's satire in
The Nabob. The opportunity for visual comedy is exploited, as Sir
Matthew presents several relics (an illegible manuscript, a green
chamberpot, some lava from Vesuvius, and a box of petrified bones,
beetles, and butterflies) to the Society, and delivers a paper on Dick
Whittington's cat. Apparently this had been the subject of a serious
dissertation actually presented to the Society in the previous year.
Dr. Samuel Pegge (not to be confused with Foote) had given a paper
on the history of Whittington which gave rise to a suggestion that
Whittington's cat may have been a slang term for a coal boat rather
than an actual animal.[8] Foote merely recognized the ludicrousness
of the topic and incorporated it into his play.

Allardyce Nicoll, one of the comparatively few scholars to have
examined the minor drama of the period, finds *The Nabob* "over-
weighted with bitterness."[9] Despite the sentimentality of the conclusion and the rather lighthearted satire on the antiquarian craze,
the play is overwhelmingly concerned with characters and activities

which illustrate the rapaciousness of man. The Nabob himself, his corrupt servants, the parasites like the procuress, Mrs. Match'em, and the waiter who is teaching Sir Matthew to gamble with *éclat*, the pocket boroughs, colonial exploitation, and the manipulation of the stock market—all these create a picture of a society in which the honest and rather guileless man like Sir John is easy prey. *The Nabob*, like *The Commissary*, has a Jonsonian bite to its satire.

Anglo-Indians were so incensed by *The Nabob* that two members of the East India Company came to call on Foote, armed with cudgels. Foote charmed them with his wit and conversation, and they stayed, first to coffee, then to dinner. The author read the manuscript aloud, assuring them that his satire was directed only at those nabobs who were corrupt. The two visitors became great patrons of the play and attended almost every performance.[10]

III The Bankrupt

The Bankrupt (1773) reflects the epidemic of business failures which recently had swept the London financial community. Some of these were believed to be fraudulent bankruptcies, simply means for avoiding the payment of debts. Belden mentions the failure of the banking firm of Neal, James, Fordyce, and Downs, much in the news the previous year.[11] The bankruptcy of Alexander Fordyce, one of the partners, is believed to have inspired Foote to write his play. But despite his involvement in the speculation which caused his firm's collapse, Fordyce was widely respected, and friends prevailed on Foote to alter his play in order to avoid further damage to Fordyce's reputation.

Foote's compliance probably accounts for the play's sentimental overtones. Sir Robert Riscounter, a city banker, is faced with ruin because his foreign bills have not been honored. Personal disgrace also threatens, for his daughter Lydia has been viciously slandered in the press and her marriage to the aristocratic Sir James Biddulph jeopardized. In *The Bankrupt*, plot controls characterization in a manner quite unusual in Foote. The scandalous allegation that Lydia has been compromised by her father's clerk originates with Lady Riscounter, Lydia's stepmother, who wishes her own daughter Lucy to marry the wealthy Sir James. This is the stuff of melodrama, or sentimental "weeping" comedy, and the characters are accordingly stereotyped. Lydia is the picture of filial duty, Lucy an acquisitive schemer interested only in finding a wealthy husband, and Lady Riscounter the archetypal stepmother, who has promised the clerk that by ruining Lydia's reputation he will eventually win her hand and fortune. Lucy admires her mother's talent for intrigue, but as Lady Riscounter points out, her natural capacity has been sharpened by education: "My father was a stock-broker, you know, and your father, my first husband, an attorney, my dear" (9).

In act 2 Sir Robert reveals his honesty and high principles by refusing to enter into false bankruptcy or to withold jewels and cash which should go toward settling his debts. This nobility of character, matched incidentally by Sir James Biddulph who never wavers in his loyalty to Lydia, would quickly pall were it not for the humor Foote has injected into his delineation of Sir Robert. In everything but business ethics he is wavering and irresolute. Lady Riscounter knows her husband's frailty:

No mortal was ever so mutable. Our various climate is not so inconstant as he. Sir Robert is choleric enough, but then, as he is provoked without cause, he is appeased without reason; one word will inflame, another extinguish the fire; whom one minute he persecutes, the next he protects. His joy, grief, love, hatred, are in eternal rotation, and I have been often tempted to think his mind a machine, moved only by the immediate objects before it. (9)

He displays his choler in ordering Lydia out of the house before ascertaining her guilt, but is as quickly appeased and convinced of her innocence.

Sir James Biddulph's clever valet, Robin, who from the beginning displays insight into the true nature of those he serves, helps to disentangle the plot by charming Kitty, the chambermaid bribed by Lady Riscounter to corroborate the slanders against Lydia. It is Robin's witty and educated manner of speaking that attracts Kitty. "What a difference between him, and the servants of this side the bar?" (3), she muses, underlining the differences between "city" and "town" which make Sir James Biddulph so desirable a husband for Lydia.

Robin is also an aspiring novelist and playwright:

Robin. For novels I have now and then some dealings with Noble, and have by me a genteel comedy of one act, that is thought to have a good deal of merit.

Kitty. And pray when does it make its appearance?
Robin. Why, faith, I don't know, all the managers are such scribblers, that
    they won't give a genius fair play, but engross the whole stage to them-
    selves. (3–4)

Foote is laughing at himself, for nearly all the plays staged at the
Haymarket were of his own writing. Garrick too had written several
successful comedies for Drury Lane, and George Colman the Elder,
manager of Covent Garden from 1767 to 1774, was a prolific dramatist. Robin's complaint is not the only instance of literary comment
in *The Bankrupt.* Foote satirized scandalmongering newspapers in
the scene where Sir Robert Riscounter and Sir James Biddulph visit
the printer's office to protest the scandalous allegations against Lydia.

In his literary endeavors, as in his courtship of Kitty, Robin may
be seen as a servant aping his betters, but the satire cuts both ways,
imputing to modern writers the intellectual prowess of servingmen.
Indeed, with servants as the subjects of novels like Richardson's
Pamela and Fielding's *Joseph Andrews,* or sentimental comic operas
like Isaac Bickerstaffe's *The Maid of the Mill,* it is only just that they
become authors as well, especially of "genteel comedy." Such an
interpretation of Robin's incongruous literary bent gains support
from the fact that Foote's other play of 1773, *The Handsome
Housemaid, or Piety in Pattens,* parodies both *Pamela* and *The Maid
of the Mill.*[12]

Numerous touches of acerbic wit redeem *The Bankrupt'*s sentimentality. Foote's exposé of fraudulent business practices in the
scene where the unscrupulous attorneys Pillage and Resource try
to influence Sir Robert is complemented by the satire on scurrilous
journalism mentioned above. The parallel between financial rumor
and malicious gossip is implicit in the disasters which threaten the
Riscounter fortune and reputation. Pillage and Resource, like the
hack writers in the printer's office, are predatory rogues who frankly
admit that their livelihood depends on the purveying of lies. The
humor consists in the ridiculousness of the deceptions foisted upon
the public. As is often true with Foote, cheats and liars thrive.

Among the morally upright characters only Sir Robert is in any
way memorable. Foote's solution to the problem of making this
high-minded banker interesting was to make him profoundly in-
consistent, vacillating wildly in his opinions as he agrees with the

most recent speaker. This changeability and his frequent choleric
outbursts serve, however, to undercut the sentimental elements
inherent in the plot.

At the end of the play Lady Riscounter's villainy is revealed. It
is the servant, Robin, who produces incriminating evidence in the
form of a note for five hundred pounds with which Lady Riscounter
has bribed Kitty. Confronted with this proof of her machinations,
and aware that Sir Robert's business is on the brink of failure, Lady
Riscounter offers no defense. Her primary concern is not moral but
financial: "Don't imagine, Sir Robert, that the provision I derive
from . . .[Lucy's] father, shall be lavished to lessen your debts, or
be employ'd in support of their autho:" (60). Lydia's willingness to
put her independent fortune at her father's disposal, and Sir James
Biddulph's offer of similar assistance meet with withering scorn from
Lady Riscounter: "Come, Lucy, let us leave these romantick creatures together, they are only fit for each other; when your effects
are convey'd to proper trustees, I shall take care to put in my claim"
(61). In true melodramatic fashion, Lady Riscounter's unlamented
departure coincides with the entrance of a clerk bearing news that
Sir Robert's foreign bills have all been honored and his bank is no
longer in danger of failing.

Lydia Riscounter, her father, and Sir James are united at the end
of the play in a new family grouping based on the same principles
of honor and integrity that Sir Robert demonstrated in his business
transactions. Even Kitty wins forgiveness, through the intercession
of Robin:

Robin. As this happy turn has been chiefly owing to Kitty, I hope she will
be restor'd to favour again.
Sir James. But consider, Robin, that was not her intention.
Robin. But recollect, Sir, the temptation—
Sir Rob. But the treachery—
Robin. Five hundred pounds.
Sir Rob. That is true—as many, her superiors, tho' perhaps not her betters,
are daily detected in doing things more criminal for less consideration,
it is some excuse, I confess. (63)

The importance of money is stressed throughout the play. Lady
Riscounter and Lucy are as devoid of moral principle as the attorneys

Pillage and Resource are of business ethics. For them, the end, financial gain, justifies the means. Lydia's engagement to Sir James typifies the role of money in the changing social structure of the eighteenth century, with members of the wealthy middle class marrying into the aristocracy. The reported failure of Sir Robert's bank is therefore a possible threat to Lydia's marriage. "You see, Sir James Biddulph," she says, "there are new obstacles oppos'd to your purpose" (61). Upward mobility in the middle class is paralleled in the case of the servants. Kitty tells Robin that the bribe of five hundred pounds will enable them "to live under our own roof, instead of that of another" (39).

Despite the stereotyped characterizations, and some rather platitudinous declarations of honor and high principle, *The Bankrupt* is not truly sentimental. Admittedly, virtue triumphs, with Sir Robert's credit restored, Lydia and Sir James united, and Robin promised a handsome reward for his honesty. These virtuous characters exist, however, within a society which seems almost totally avaricious and dishonest. Moral probity is possible, in this world, but it is by no means the norm.

In *The Maid of Bath, The Nabob,* and *The Bankrupt,* vice is exposed, but not really punished. Even the happy endings are so obviously imposed as to reveal the powerlessness of Foote's "good" characters. There is a realistic touch in these, as in many of his plays: an almost characteristic moment of moral ambiguity when the villain retires unrepentant and unchastized, suggesting that neither moral nor social censure can affect the hardened reprobate. Power resides in money, not in virtue.

CHAPTER 10

The Last Plays—Bitter Jests

I   The Cozeners

IN his last three plays Foote returned again to the bitter tone of Jonsonian satire. *The Cozeners* (1774) is yet another study of the predatory element in society. The following year he decided to capitalize on the notoriety of the Duchess of Kingston, and wrote *A Trip to Calais* in which she was satirized as Lady Kitty Crocodile. A savage dispute developed between Foote and the Duchess, whose influence was sufficiently great to prevent the play being licensed by the Lord Chamberlain. It was never acted. Later, Foote revised *A Trip to Calais,* and the altered play, *The Capuchin,* was performed in 1776. Actual events and persons have a significance in these plays unusual even for Foote, who habitually relied on topical satire.

The Cozeners is undeniably one of the most derivative of Foote's plays. It is indebted generally to Jonson's *Alchemist* and, for the material of one scene, to Vanbrugh's *Confederacy.*[1] In addition, it owes much to Foote's own works. Aircastle is related to the garrulous Sir Penurious Trifle in *The Knights,*[2] and Toby Aircastle, the lumpish son, is a descendant of Tim Gazette in the same play. The similarities between certain situations and characters in *The Knights* and Goldsmith's *She Stoops to Conquer* have been noted in chapter 2, and the resemblance of Aircastle and his son Toby to Hardcastle and Tony Lumpkin suggests that Foote was reclaiming Goldsmith's borrowings. The basic plot is reminiscent of *The Commissary.* Mrs. Fleece'em and her partner, attorney Flaw, gull their clients, including the Aircastles, as Mrs. Mechlin had fleeced Zachary Fungus in the earlier play. An unscrupulous marriage broker, Felicia Fleece'em, also recalls Mrs. Match'em in *The Nabob* and Mrs. Cole in *The Minor.*

To these ingredients drawn from other plays Foote added his usual seasoning of incidents and personalities from the London

110

scene. He fashioned this multiplicity into a surprisingly unified play. It is distinguished by the presence of some of his best characters, and by a well-constructed plot. *The Cozeners* encapsulates his view of London as the hunting ground for predators and cheats, and underlines the manifest ridiculousness of the various credulous cits and country bumpkins who are their natural prey.

Flaw and Mrs. Fleece'em, the cozeners, have combined to form a kind of business agency for the purpose of bilking the public. Their partnership is underpinned by a contract, the terms of which constitute a charter for fraud. Flaw has provided credit enabling Mrs. Fleece'em to take a mansion in the fashionable "town" and employ servants suitable to such a household. Having established Mrs. Fleece'em as a person of substance, Flaw covenants to circulate in private gatherings and public places, and in the press, that the lady's powerful connections enable her "to procure posts, places, preferments . . . to raise cash for the indigent, and procure good securities for such as are wealthy; suitable matches for people who want husbands and wives, and divorces for those who wish to get rid of them" (6–7).

The other factor binding the pair together, as the wrangling at the beginning of the play illustrates, is Flaw's hold over Mrs. Fleece'em. Formerly transported to America for theft, she has returned before her time, so Flaw can blackmail her into raising his percentage of the profits.

Mrs. Fleece'em cunningly gives the impression of being patronized by fashionable society. Flaw has bribed a coachman "to parade before . . . [her] house for an hour, after his master is set down at the Cockpit. A couple of servants . . . wait at the door, as if the great man was above" (10). Complimentary cards bearing the names of dukes, earls, and viscounts also have been provided by Flaw, to be conspicuously displayed on the mantelpiece. For her part, Mrs. Fleece'em has her servants tell visitors who call in her absence that she is out with the Countess of Carnaby, "to see the preparations for the great trial in Westminster Hall' (26), a reference to the trial of the Duchess of Kingston on charges of bigamy. Foote's pair of cheats are clever and greedy, with a sharp eye for human weakness. They are as ready to cozen one another as to fleece their victims.

The first of these victims is O'Flannagan, newly arrived from Limerick. His presence in England reflects the endemic poverty of Ireland, which provided a steady flow of cheap labor for Britain and the new world. The exploitation of the Irish is satirized in the nonexistent positions Mrs. Fleece'em promises to O'Flannagan—collector of window-lights in the Falkland Islands, or surveyorship of the woods there (references to the remote and barren islands for control of which Spain and England nearly had gone to war in late 1769). As O'Flannagan suffers from seasickness he requests a different post and is offered "a tidewaiter's place in the inland part of America" (13). Tidewaiters, being customs officers who go on board ship, would hardly be employed inland. In any case, as indicated by Flaw's remark that a free coat of tar and feathers is one of the perquisites of the job, customs officials were decidedly unpopular in America during this period of protest against British taxation. Nevertheless, the Irishman readily offers a bribe in order to secure such a position.

O'Flannagan, one of Foote's best stage Irishmen, possesses in abundance the comic characteristics usually attributed to his countrymen in the eighteenth century: ignorance, illogicality, and a gift for conversation. Ireland is deserted, he reports, since so many have emigrated: "In a hundred miles riding, I did not meet with a human cratur, except sheep and oxen, to tell me the road; and I should have lost myself again and again, but for the mile-stones, that are so kind to answer your questions without giving you the trouble to ask them: And so, being desirous to follow my neighbours' example, I have, madam, made bold to come over before them" (12). At the end of the play, O'Flannagan, who prevents Mrs. Fleece'em's escape and retrieves his money, has learned enough to realize that his best plan is "to make an emigration back to Ireland again" (76).

In Moses Manassas, a wealthy moneylender who is the cozeners' second victim, Foote satirized Jewish efforts to enter fashionable society. Moses' aspirations are reflected in expensive though bizarre clothing, and in his adoption of the sports favored by the aristocracy. He has even ridden in a horse race, though his noble opponent won by foul play, pushing Moses from his horse, much to the entertainment of the crowd. Flaw flatters Manassas on his success with women. The suggestion that his singing attracts them is made laughable when Moses demonstrates his talent in a dreadful voice and heavy accent.

The entire satire on the Jew is dependent upon the impossibility of his being accepted in society. His business with Flaw and Mrs.

Fleece'em involves their rigging the ballot so he can become a member of Boodle's or Almack's, the fashionable gaming clubs where he has previously been blackballed. Moses assumes he has been barred from membership because of his religion, though Mrs. Fleece'em's suggestion that the club members are so much in his debt that they cannot afford to give him access to their favorite haunts has some truth in it. "So you have been admitted into the Jerusalem Chamber!" (17) she cries, a satirical thrust at Charles James Fox, who was at this period so much in debt to Jewish moneylenders that he referred to the outer room of his apartments as the "Jerusalem Chamber."[3]

The satire reflects the growing importance of Jewish financial interests in London. Foote shows no sympathy for the Jews, and is anti-Semitic in so far as he finds their desire to enter society a fit subject for ridicule. In view of the prevalent antipathy toward Jews in the 1770s, however, the satire is mild. Moses Manassas may be a caricature of some particular Jew whose eccentricities of dress and pursuit of women had drawn Foote's notice. Whether those details are based on mimicry or on original invention, the resulting characterization is sufficiently multifaceted to avoid the stereotypes of racial humor.

Foote illustrates the scope of Flaw's and Mrs. Fleece'em's endeavors by having them first accept O'Flannagan's bribe, then several sheets of lottery tickets (as good as cash) from Manassas. Reported frauds include taking money from a young ensign to whom they have promised promotion, and an employment-agency scheme which provides the pair with commissions from both job seeker and employer. They also undertake the sale of parliamentary seats, and expect good business when the first ships arrive from Tanjore, a reference to the wealth and influence of the nabobs. Their range implies a pervasively corrupt society.

Finally, Mrs. Fleece'em and Flaw are given a bank draft for one hundred pounds by Mrs. Simony, the gossipy, name-dropping wife of a clergyman who is hoping for her husband's appointment to a lucrative position in the church. The Simony incident, discussed below, was a direct reference to a recent scandal.

The cozeners' method is to accept bribes for nonexistent positions or for favors they are powerless to grant. Mrs. Fleece'em, however, also shows considerable initiative in acquiring goods by fraudulent means. Obtaining expensive silks from a London mercer, Paul Prig, she carries him off in her carriage to receive payment from her "lawyer," really a Dr. Hellebore, noted for treating madmen. Privately informed by Mrs. Fleece'em that Prig is her uncle who suffers from serious delusions, the latest being that he is a mercer on Ludgate Hill, Hellebore questions Prig and then has him seized and carried away for treatment in his Chelsea asylum. This incredible incident also was taken from current London gossip.

There are two main strands to Foote's plot in *The Cozeners*. First there is the cozening itself, represented by Mrs. Fleece'em and Flaw who demonstrate their virtuosity in the techniques of bribery and fraud. The second is centered on the Aircastles, a country family come to London to find a rich wife for their loutish son Toby. The two strands of the plot meet when the Aircastles are caught by the cozeners through Flaw's arranging a tentative match with a "West Indian heiress," supposedly Mrs. Fleece'em's niece but in reality a black servant named Marianne whom she has brought back with her from America.

Foote's treatment of the Aircastles encompasses social satire on topics ranging from family relationships and arranged marriages to female chastity. Ignorant, yet each convinced of his superior wisdom, Mr. and Mrs. Aircastle bicker constantly. Proof of their judgment is their lodging in a bagnio, or brothel, mistaken for an hotel. Innocence combines with ignorance to make them typically vulnerable country boobies. Even Tom, the waiter in the bagnio, finds their uncouth behavior intolerable, complaining that "it is one eternal wrangle between them, conducted in a language pretty near as coarse as their carter's." Flaw's excuse for their conduct, "They have been bred in a state of Nature, Tom" (28), is almost certainly a passing jibe at Rousseau's celebration of the virtues of natural man.

On his wife's advice Aircastle has sold a parcel of land in Wiltshire. The proceeds of the sale are to help Toby to a wealthy wife, for whom Mrs. Aircastle intends to advertise: "Wanted for a young gentleman of an ancient family, and agreeable person. . . . A wife with a very large portion: If the fortune answers, proper allowance will be made for person and mind. The party, and his rent-roll, may be seen at the Lamb in Long-Acre, every hour of the day" (32–33). The Aircastle's view of marriage as a financial transaction reflects accepted social practice. In his previous play, *The Bankrupt*, Foote

had made the hypocritical daughter, Lucy, spokesman for this philosophy: "For instance now, Sir Thomas Perkins, our neighbour,
finding that Miss Williams has a good parcel of land, which being
contiguous to his estate, will be very proper for him to possess;
immediately sends his rent-roll a–courting to her's. The parchments
are produced on both sides, and no impediments, that is incum-
brance appearing, a couple of lawyers marry the manors together"
(19). Lucy's cynical acceptance of the arranged marriage is scorned
by Lydia Riscounter as mere "barter and sale." It is barter and sale
the Aircastles rely on to secure the supposed West Indian heiress
for their son. At Flaw's insistence expensive gifts are purchased for
the intended bride, and a generous settlement proposed for Mrs.
Fleece'em.

Toby, described by his father as "just like a spider, nothing but
legs" (59), is awkward, uncouth, and stupid. His natural doltishness
is emphasized by outlandish clothes chosen by his mother. Toby
is dimly aware of the incongruous result of this parental care: "I
don't understand what father and mother's about. Here am I di-
zened, and skewered, and graced, just like a young colt that is a-
breaking: Nay, they were going to advertise me too, as if I was
really a horse; but lawyer Flaw has made them alter their minds,
and I am to be disposed of by private contract, I think" (44). The
proposed marriage does not greatly trouble Toby, though he sighs
for his former love, Betsy Blossom,[4] a country girl he has debauched.
Unknown to the Aircastles, Betsy, now a whore in the bagnio where
they lodge, attempts to trick Toby into marriage. Easily deluded
by her transparently melodramatic protestations that she will die
unless he marries her, Toby willingly agrees. But his loyalty is of
short duration. Wooing the Negro girl Marianne in a darkened
room, he is much impressed with the softness of her skin and with
her amiability. The surprise occasioned by seeing Marianne in day-
light, however, sends him scuttling back to Betsy. Toby's prospec-
tive brides reflect his own lack of judgment; the first a whore and
a second a poor, ignorant black servant. The implication is that any
female would satisfy Toby, who responds to women only on a physical level. Such is man in a state of nature.

Mr. Aircastle is characterized by extreme garrulousness and an
inability to confine himself to the topic. Beneath his eccentric manner he is a sensible if rather conservative country squire, very like

Goldsmith's Hardcastle in his preference for the country over the town, and in his dislike for current fashion. He is painfully aware of Toby's shortcomings and of the ludicrous figure he cuts in his modish finery. There is a suggested model for Foote's portrait in one Gagahan, an Irishman, but the style of Gagahan's own prose character of Foote, written after Foote's death, does not resemble that of the "prolix and digressive" Aircastle.[5] Indeed, the rapidity with which one topic is superseded by the next in Aircastle's speech suggests that the technique of *reductio ad absurdum* has been applied to Locke's theory of the association of ideas. Sterne of course had set a precedent for this kind of parody in *Tristram Shandy* some years earlier.

Foote may have taken some of Mrs. Aircastle's traits from Wycherley's *The Country Wife*.[6] As ignorant and as lustful as Margery Pinchwife, Elizabeth Aircastle is in her own way a cozener as well. On arrival in London she has written to an admirer, Colonel Gorget, intimating that she would not prove ungrateful if he were to lend her five hundred guineas: "If Colonel Gorget answers my letter in the way I expect, it will prove a pretty good beginning: The colonel, I make no doubt, knows the ways of the world, and will soon take the hint: He was vastly struck with me during the races; and I don't see why I have not as good a right to profit by my person, as I am told some ladies do" (37–38). By chance, Gorget meets Aircastle and borrows the money from him. Aircastle, unaware of the lady's identity, proclaims that no woman is worth that price and contributes the blunt advice that he should endeavor to get her for nothing. The woman is a cormorant, says Aircastle, and deserves to be "choused," which is to say swindled.

Foote demonstrates how cozening permeates this sexual escapade. The seduction takes place—at least, when the lovers are interrupted by Toby, Mrs. Aircastle quickly suggests that they remove to the room overhead, where she can furnish the Colonel with a receipt for his money. Colonel Gorget does avoid paying, since he presents the husband's money to the erring wife, though he redeems himself considerably at the end of the play by retrieving the Aircastles' money from Mrs. Fleece'em and Flaw.

Mrs. Aircastle's hypocrisy and lack of principle parody the sentiments in Lord Chesterfield's letters to his son, on which she has based Toby's training. Mr. Aircastle, however, is dubious:

Air. Grace! he has neither grace, nor grease: his breast-bone sticks out like a turkey's.

Mrs. Air. Nothing but grace! I wish you would read some late Posthumous Letters; you would then know the true value of grace: Do you know, that the only way for a young man to thrive in the world, is to get a large dish of hypocrisy, well garnished with grace, an agreeable person, and a clear patrimonial estate? (33)

Constant exhortations to remember "grace" prove particularly unsuccessful with the loutish Toby. Foote's jibe at Chesterfield's letters is less ambitious than the proposed satire which had met with Samuel Johnson's approval,[7] though it does underline the worldliness and lack of sincerity deplored by Chesterfield's critics.

In *The Cozeners* Foote aired a number of the skeletons in the cupboards of London society. Belden has discussed in detail most of the incidents he incorporated into the play.[8] It is useful, however, to look briefly at some of these scandals. A Mrs. Grieve who, like Mrs. Fleece'em, had been transported claimed kinship with Lord North and with the Duke of Grafton, and gave credibility to the relationships by bribing Lord North's porter to admit her to his house. She acted as a marriage broker, in this capacity duping Charles James Fox, to whom she promised a West Indian heiress, Miss Phipps. Mrs. Grieve advanced Fox money, supposedly part of the Phipps fortune, and in return arranged that his carriage should be seen frequently outside her door. The parallel with Mrs. Fleece'em's ruses is obvious. Toby Aircastle's courtship of the black servant Marianne also ridicules Fox, who according to rumor, like Toby had to powder his eyebrows to please his dark lady. Another of Mrs. Fleece'em's exploits, added to the play in 1776,[9] was the gulling of Prig the mercer. This was based on a fraud reputedly perpetrated by the notorious Mrs. Margaret Caroline Rudd, who in 1775 was tried for forgery and acquitted, though her supposed accomplices, the Perreaus, were hanged.

Mrs. Simony's bribing of Flaw and Mrs. Fleece'em with a "hymn" (to the tune of one hundred pounds) composed by her preacher husband directly parallels a recent attempt by the wife of Dr. William Dodd, chaplain of the Magdalen Hospital in London, to bribe Lady Apsley, the Lord Chancellor's wife, and thereby obtain for her husband the living of St. George's, Hanover Square. Dodd claimed to know nothing of the affair, though that did not prevent his name being struck off the list of the King's chaplains.

Clearly, in *The Cozeners* the most amusing and preposterous incidents are taken from life. Foote's use of so much contemporary material in this play carries the implication, in fact, that his dramatic satire is here intended to reflect fairly closely the society in which he lived. Certainly this wider application is borne out by the closing lines of the play, spoken by Mrs. Fleece'em: "I am detected, distressed, and must therefore submit! But, gentlemen, if all who have offended like us, were like us produced to the public, much higher names would adorn the Old Bailey Chronicle than those of poor Fleece'em and Flaw!" (77).

The prevalence of bribery and political patronage in eighteenth-century life is matched by the universal corruption in *The Cozeners*. Everyone in the play is to some extent a cozener, even the victims like the ensign, O'Flannagan, Moses Manassas, and Mrs. Simony, who seek advancement not through merit but by bribery. Marriages too are based on deception. Aircastle is blind to his wife's infidelity. She dupes her husband by selling herself to Colonel Gorget, who in turn bilks her, and enjoys her for nothing. Betsy Blossom feigns love for Toby, and though he has earlier debauched her, she forfeits sympathy by resorting to deceit. The Aircastle money no doubt heightens her affection. She too has been cheated, however, when the Aircastles, wanting Toby to marry money, used their influence to drive her from the parish. Fittingly, it is the financial aspect of Toby's marriage that makes the Aircastles easy prey for Flaw and Mrs. Fleece'em.

Even Mrs. Fleece'em's activities in America are seen as a kind of cozening: "Did not my burning the first pound of Souchong, and my speeches at Faneuil-Hall, and the Liberty-Tree, against the colonies contributing to discharge a debt to which they owe their existence, procure me the love and esteem of the people?" (6). The American desire for independence is portrayed as an attempt by the colonists to cheat England of tax revenue, and to evade their share of the debt incurred in the defense of their country during the Seven Years War. Because of the licensing laws Foote rarely indulged in political satire, but a slur on the motives of the Americans was eminently acceptable to the British government in 1774.

In *The Cozeners* greed dominates public and private life. Marriage partners are sold, as Toby says, like horses. Women turn natural lasciviousness to financial advantage, and Mrs. Aircastle is no less a whore than Betsy Blossom. No one in the play refuses a bribe or balks at paying one. Corruption is the norm. The world of the play mirrors the complicated structure of patronage, intrigue, and bribery which is a commonplace of eighteenth-century political and social history. Despite the abundance of topical allusion, *The Cozeners* is a wide-ranging general satire on contemporary life.

II   A Trip to Calais

A Trip to Calais was written for the 1775 summer season at the Haymarket, but never performed. In it Foote made capital out of two scandalous incidents which had recently engrossed the public's attention. More scandal was to follow, in the form of a vicious smear campaign aimed at Foote. For this reason, the factual background of *A Trip to Calais* is particularly important.

Foote based the plot of his play on the elopement of Richard Brinsley Sheridan and Elizabeth Linley.[10] Miss Linley, whom Foote had earlier portrayed as Kitty Linnet in *The Maid of Bath*, fled to France in March, 1772, with Sheridan and a chaperon, in order to escape the attentions of Matthews (Rackett in *The Maid of Bath*), an importunate suitor. In Calais she and Sheridan were married, though they kept the marriage a secret. Miss Linley took sanctuary in a religious house in Lille. Her father came to France in April and was reconciled with his daughter and Sheridan, but insisted that Elizabeth return with him to Bath and continue her singing career. In April, 1773, Miss Linley again married Sheridan, who in the interim had fought two widely publicized duels with Matthews. The couple became the darlings of aristocratic society, and in 1775 Sheridan was very much in the public eye as a result of his theatrical successes, his first great comedy, *The Rivals*, and *The Duenna*, a comic opera.

There is no evidence that Jenny Minnikin in Foote's play, the selfish and forward daughter of a pinmaker who elopes with her father's apprentice, Dicky Drugget, resembles Elizabeth Linley in any respect but the circumstantial details of the elopement. Miss Linley was universally admired and respected for the sweetness of her nature, as well as her beauty and voice.[11] Jenny Minnikin, on the other hand, is pert, common, and wilful. Nor is there much of Sheridan in Dicky Drugget, who in any case appears only in the first scene of the play. Jenny's defense of Dicky, however, as having no vices "except lying out all night now and then, . . . frequenting the tavern in search of good company, [and] running his father in debt for his credit" (8), probably alludes to Sheridan's general conviviality, his gallantry with the ladies, and his invariably precarious financial state. Before Dicky and Jenny can find a parson to marry them word comes that the Minnikin family has arrived in pursuit of their wayward daughter. Jenny seeks the protection of the abbess in a nearby convent, while Dicky escapes to another town.

The remainder of the plot is unrelated to the Sheridan–Linley elopement. Their attempts to remove Jenny from the convent having failed, the Minnikins take the advice of a fraudulent priest, O'Donnovan, and ask Lady Kitty Crocodile, an Englishwoman living in Calais, for assistance. Lady Kitty, whose tyranny has caused both her maid and companion to revolt, recognizes in the rebellious and selfish Jenny a kindred spirit, and offers her a position in her household. Poetic justice is served, for, as the former maid remarks, the two "will prove a mutual plague to each other" (74).

In *A Trip to Calais* Foote satirized tradesmen, creating a gallery of cits as varied as those in *The Mayor of Garratt*. Mr. Minnikin and his wife are typical novice travelers. Mrs. Minnikin complains bitterly about the roughness of the crossing and the inadequacy of the accommodation on board ship. Both are violently anti-Papist, and, on the strength of their journey from customs house to hotel, vastly unimpressed with France. Their choice of husband for Jenny, a fishmonger named Kit Codling, has accompanied them, noting in his diary for future publication the most tedious details of his travels. Codling's observations, and Mrs. Minnikin's remark that "his'n may be as useful as many of the Voyages that have been printed of late" (19), are satiric references to the recent proliferation of voyage narratives.[12]

Foote extends the satire on tradesmen abroad in the character of the milliner Mrs. Clack, Jenny Minnikin's aptly named aunt. Unlike the rest of her family she has moved her business to fashionable Pall Mall and prides herself on her superiority to the "mere cits" who are ignorant of what goes on in the world. The French are so much more clever than the English, asserts Mrs. Clack, that even mere infants here "sputter French, more freer and glibber" (20) than Jenny Minnikin, who was five years at the Swiss French boarding school in North London.

An even more amusing Francophile is Luke Lapelle, a Bond Street tailor. He and his wife have journeyed from Paris with the Minnikins' neighbors, Mrs. and Mrs. Gingham. Minnikin's hearty greeting, "Well met neighbour Gingham! What, you've been fetching home fashions, I reckon?" (21), is sharply rebuked, for the travelers have been treated like nobility by the French and have no wish to proclaim their trade. The price of being taken for lords is high, as Gingham confesses, nor did they dispute the bills, because "we wa'n't willing to bring a disgrace on our dignity" (22).

In his travels, Lapelle has acquired if not mastered a vocabulary of French phrases. He always avoids the English abroad. "There's a roughness, a *bourgoisy*, about our barbarians, that is not at all to my taste; not a bit, as the French say, to my *gout*" (24). Questioned on the health of the royal family, he reports that "Mr. *le Roi*, as the French say, looked pretty jolly" (24). Lapelle's supreme affectation is to refer to his wife as Mademoiselle, and make her pass for his mistress, since "nothing can be so vulgar in France, as voyaging about with one's wife" (26).

Cits like the Minnikins are insular and ignorant, their pretentious counterparts from the town only slightly less so. As in *The Englishman in Paris* and its sequel, the satire is directed both at those who can find nothing to admire in France, and those who with a superficial understanding of French culture become slavishly Francophile. The cits represent not just tradesmen but the growing middle class, merchants, bankers, and manufacturers, rapidly gaining influence, and metaphorically moving to the town during the period. What established society saw as their pretentiousness and vulgarity is magnified in Foote's treatment. Similarly, he burlesques the Sheridan elopement by diminishing the lovers' social standing. There is nothing romantic about Jenny and Dicky—they are self-willed and silly. So, perhaps, were the original lovers, though by 1775 they had transcended their earlier difficulties, and were courted by the leaders of fashionable society.

Religious hypocrisy is also satirized in *A Trip to Calais*. The abbess of the convent to which Jenny has fled is as eager to obtain the girl's dowry as her soul. Foote casts her interview with Jenny in the form of a catechism, the abbess recommending a spiritual spouse while Jenny proclaims her fondness for the flesh and blood variety. Although her religious instruction is sound enough, the revelation that her pupil has no private income prompts the abbess

to conclude hastily that Jenny has no vocation and should therefore
return to her father. Unwilling to comply, Jenny employs the few
guineas in her possession to buy the abbess's protection.

The other representative of corruption within the church is
O'Donnovan, an Irish laborer who passes in France for a Capuchin
(Franciscan) friar, and circumvents his vow of poverty by accepting
money only in a purse so his hands need not touch it. It is he who
advises the Minnikins to enlist the help of Lady Kitty Crocodile,
for if he were to assist in getting Jenny out of the convent he would
surely "be guilty of sacredness" (32). Although O'Donnovan and the
abbess are both inclined to be avaricious, they offer harm to no one,
and the satire is in consequence rather mild. O'Donnovan, indeed,
is somewhat endearing, posing as a mendicant friar not because he
dislikes work but "only because it is so very laborious" (30).

The major scandal to which Foote alludes in *A Trip to Calais*
involved the Duchess of Kingston. As Elizabeth Chudleigh, maid
of honor to the Princess of Wales, she had charmed many courtiers,
rumor including even George II among her admirers. Her marriage
to Augustus John Hervey was kept secret so she could continue in
her position as maid of honor. In 1747 the birth of a son to Miss
Chudleigh was common gossip at court. Her behavior was invariably
scandalous. She once attended the Venetian ambassador's masquerade as Iphigenia, costumed only in a transparent veil and a
girdle of leaves, murmuring as she made her entrance that she was
"ready for the sacrifice."[13]

Eventually Elizabeth Chudleigh became the Duke of Kingston's
mistress and, aspiring to a title, arranged that her former marriage
be declared invalid. It is suspected that the Duke bribed her husband, Hervey, on this occasion. Miss Chudleigh succeeded in becoming Duchess of Kingston and reportedly lived quite happily
with the Duke until his death in 1773. The terms of his will gave
the Duchess nearly all his fortune. His sister's son, Evelyn Mead-
ows, formerly the Duke's heir, received only 500 pounds. He produced evidence of the Duchess's first marriage and on December
10, 1774, she was indicted on a charge of bigamy. In the meantime,
Hervey had succeeded his brother as Earl of Bristol, so Miss Chudleigh, if not Duchess of Kingston, would be the Countess of Bristol,
an important consideration, for the title assured her of the right to
be tried before the House of Lords and meant that even if convicted
of bigamy she would not be branded on the hand. On her return

from a visit to Rome, where she had been entertained by the pope, the Duchess learned of the charge against her and at once fled across the Channel to Calais, where she remained for two months working feverishly with her lawyers to prepare her defense before finally returning to England.[14] Hence the significance of Calais in Foote's play.

Her flamboyant nature and the publicity accorded her adventures made the Duchess of Kingston a natural target for Foote's satire. In Lady Kitty Crocodile she is caricatured as a hypocritical and malicious widow much given to public displays of inconsolable grief for her late husband. These Crocodile tears and her affectionate concern for her companion Lydia when guests are present conceal the jealous virago whose greatest pleasure is to tyrannize over her household.

Lady Kitty's excessive and very public mourning, her ill-treatment of her companion, Lydia Lydell, her advice to Jenny that a girl unable to choose between suitors should marry both, the setting in Calais, and even the visit to the pope are direct allusions to the Duchess of Kingston. Foote may have obtained information from Lydia's counterpart, a Miss Penrose, who had been treated badly by the Duchess and had consequently left her service.[15]

Mrs. Clack, as former milliner to Lady Kitty, is the Minnikins' emissary to her ladyship. Foote uses her to direct further sallies at the Duchess. The first of these refers to her marriage, after almost twenty years as his mistress, to the Duke of Kingston. It was Mrs. Clack, Lady Kitty recalls, who dressed her for the wedding, decking her out "like another Iphigenia, to be sacrificed at the temple of Hymen" (58), an allusion to the sensation the Duchess had created at the Venetian ambassador's masquerade. Lady Kitty's hypocritical pretense of innocence is caricatured in Mrs. Clack's account of the wedding night: "Your ladyship shewed a becoming coyness upon the occasion. I remember, about the hour of bedding, you hid yourself behind the bottle-rack in the beer cellar, to avoid Sir John; if your ladyship had not happened to have coughed, we should not have found you" (58). The milliner also remembers how Lady Kitty's grief was assuaged when she first tried on her widow's weeds, "and no wonder, for it is a dress vastly becoming, especially to people inclined to be fat" (38). Another incident concerning a letter from Lord Harry Huntwidow, delivered by Mrs. Clack, alludes to the Duchess's many admirers. There is a strong suggestion in the play that sexual jealousy is behind Lady Kitty's ill–treatment of Lydia. In a violent outburst she accuses her companion of impropriety with the late Lord John, and of attempting to ensnare her admirers in Italy. Even the rudimentary romantic interest in *A Trip to Calais* is linked with Lady Kitty's jealousy. Colonel Crosby is in love with Lydia, and the knowledge that any man could prefer Lydia's company to her own is galling to Lady Kitty. When the couple announce that they will marry and return to England, she flies into a temper and slanders them both.

Foote's barbs are directed at the Duchess's character rather than at her uncertain marital state. Her hypocritical displays of grief are coupled with so insistent a need for masculine admiration that unreasoning jealousy is the result. It is a cruel though perhaps accurate portrait of a hoydenish former beauty grown fat and common.

III   *The Duchess's Revenge*

While awaiting trial the Duchess learned that Foote intended to caricature her in his forthcoming play, and used her influence to prevent *A Trip to Calais* being licensed. Very likely she also had access to the play while it was in the Lord Chamberlain's hands. Unable to stage the play upon which he had relied for his summer's earnings, Foote threatened to publish it with a dedication to the Duchess.[16] They met but reached no agreement. At one point the Duchess offered 150 pounds, the printer's price, for the play. Foote scoffed at this as inadequate compensation for the box-office receipts lost because the play was banned. He accused the Duchess of bribery and was in turn accused of blackmail. During the summer of 1775 they conducted an acrimonious public correspondence, recounted in detail by both Belden and Trefman.[17] Their letters contributed as much to the public's entertainment as Foote's play would have done.

During this dispute vicious attacks against Foote appeared in the press. A campaign to destroy the actor's reputation was engineered by the journalist Dr. William Jackson, who has been identified by Belden as the Duchess of Kingston's secretary, though according to Peter Stuart, who knew the man well, Jackson was not acquainted with the Duchess, and became involved in her quarrel with Foote "because he was cunning and mercenary and the Duchess foolish and wealthy." Stuart reports that Jackson received an ample reward

from the Duchess. [18] Jackson used his position as editor of *The Public
Ledger* to spread rumors that Foote was homosexual. Other papers
naturally repeated the innuendo. It is to these rumors and the
allegations of blackmail that Foote refers in a conciliatory letter to
the Duchess, dated August 13, 1775. Explaining that a member of
the privy council has informed him that publication of *A Trip to
Calais* might at this point be injurious to the Duchess's affairs, he
offers to completely suppress the play provided the attacks in the
newspapers cease.

The Duchess's refusal is couched in language which reveals the
accuracy of Foote's depiction of her as Lady Kitty Crocodile:

Sir,
   I *was* at dinner when I received your ill-judged letter. As there is little
consideration required, I shall sacrifice a few moments to answer it.
   A member of *your* privy council can never hope to be of a Lady's cabinet.
I know too well what is due to my own dignity, to enter into a compromise
with an extortionable assassin of private reputation. If I before abhorred
you for your slander, I now despise you for your concessions. It is a proof
of the illiberality of your satire, when you can publish, or suppress it as
best suits the needy convenience of your purse. You first had the cowardly
baseness to draw the sword; and if I sheathe it until I make you crouch like
the subservient vassal you are, then is there not spirit in an injured woman,
nor meanness in a slanderous buffoon.
   To a man, my sex alone would have screened me from attack; but I am
writing to the descendant of a Merry Andrew, and prostitute the term of
manhood by applying it to Mr. Foote.
   Clothed in my innocence as in a coat of mail, I am proof against a host
of foes; and, conscious of never having intentionally offended a single individual, I doubt not that a brave and generous public will protect me from
the malevolence of a theatrical assassin. . . .
   There is something however in your *pity* at which my nature revolts. To
make an offer of pity, at once betrays your insolence and your vanity. I
will keep the *pity* you send, until the morning before you are turned off:
when I will return it by a Cupid with a box of lip-salve; and a choir of
choristers shall chaunt a stave to your *requiem.*
                                                            E. Kingston.
   Kingston House
   Sunday, 13th August.
P.S. You would have received this sooner, but the servant has been a long
time writing it.

   At no loss to reply to such an ill-bred scold, Foote seized upon her protestation of innocence and her rather injudicious introduction of the verb "prostitute" in a witty recapitulation of her past exploits:

Madam,
Though I have neither time nor inclination to answer the illiberal attacks of your agents, yet a public correspondence with your Grace is too great an honour for me to decline.

I cannot help thinking that it would have been prudent in your Grace to have answered my letter *before dinner*, or at least postponed it to the cool hour of the morning: you would then have found that I had voluntarily granted the request which you had endeavoured by so many different ways to obtain. . . .

But why, Madam, put on your *coat of mail* against me? I have no hostile intentions. Folly, not vice, is the game I pursue. In those scenes which you so unaccountably apply to yourself, you must observe there is not the slightest hint at the little incidents of your life which have excited the *curiosity* of the grand inquest for the county of Middlesex. I am happy however, Madam, to hear that your robe of innocence is in such perfect repair: I was afraid it might be a little the worse for wearing. May it hold out to keep your Grace warm the next winter.

The progenitors your Grace has done me the honour to give me, are, I presume, merely metaphorical persons; and to be considered as the authors of my muse, and not of my manhood. A Merry Andrew and a prostitute are no bad poetical parents, especially for a writer of plays: the first to give the humour and mirth; the last to furnish the graces and powers of attraction. Prostitutes, and players too, must live by pleasing the public; not but your Grace may have heard of ladies who by *private practice* have accumulated great fortunes. . . .

I am obliged to your Grace for your intended present "on the day" (as you *politely* express it) "when I am to be turned off." But where will your Grace get the *Cupid* to bring me the lip-salve? That family, I am afraid, has long quitted *your* service.

Pray, Madam, is not J. . . n the name of your *female* confidential secretary? And is not *she* generally clothed in black petticoats made of your weeds?

"So mourned the dame of Ephesus her love!"

I fancy your Grace took the hint when you last resided at Rome. You heard then, I suppose, of a certain pope; and in humble imitation, have converted a *pious parson* into a *chamber-maid*. The scheme is new in this country; and has, doubtless, its particular pleasures. That you may *never want the benefit of the clergy* in every emergence, is the sincere wish of

> Your Grace's most devoted,
> Most obliged humble servant,
> Sam. Foote.[19]

Foote's letter reveals his superiority in the paper war. This rare example of Foote speaking in his own voice indicates the strength of his polished, incisive prose, as excellent in its way as the wittiest of his dramatic characterizations.

Nonetheless, the attacks continued unabated in the press. In the spring of 1776, Foote, very upset by the allegations, also feared that they might provoke harsh treatment from his audiences during the forthcoming summer season. Taking the advice of his friends, he opened the Haymarket on May 20, 1776, and when the curtain was raised, addressed the audience. Their applause for his speech, and throughout the performance of *The Bankrupt,* was evidence of their support and sympathy. His choice of this play was particularly felicitous, both for its satire on scandalmongering newspaper hacks, and because it was *The Bankrupt* which Foote had voluntarily revised to avoid unjustly maligning another man's reputation.

Early in the summer the allegations of homosexuality were given substance when John Sangster, a servant Foote had discharged, was encouraged by Jackson to accuse his former master of criminal assault. It was not until December of that year that Foote was able to bring the case to court and vindicate his reputation. When Foote heard that the jury had returned a verdict of "Not Guilty," he fell into a state of hysterical collapse, and could not for an entire hour be made to understand the good news.[20]

IV The Capuchin

The strain had been severe. During the summer Foote had revised *A Trip to Calais* entitling it *The Capuchin* and introducing a satire on Jackson in the character of Dr. Viper, a fraudulent priest and former muckraking journalist. His evident bitterness toward Jackson distorts the play, making it less entertaining than the original. Dr. Viper is not one of Foote's memorable eccentrics, but a villain whose proper dramatic province is melodrama. O'Donnovan, played by Foote, had known Viper in London. The two rogues, both disguised as clergymen, meet in Calais. In the course of an argument O'Donnovan outlines Viper's miserable career; expelled as parish clerk to a Moravian meetinghouse for robbing the poor box, dismissed as a bill-sticker for selling the bills as waste paper, and at last jailed as a swindler. Viper's most recent occupation in England is an allusion to Jackson and the Duchess of Kingston: "Then you became doer of the Scandalous Chronicle; mowed down reputations like muck; pushed yourself into the pay of lady Deborah Dripping, produced anonymous paragraphs against her of your own composition, and got paid by her for not putting them into your paper" (92). Foote's satire on irresponsible journalism in *The Capuchin* is a direct response to Jackson's libels.

The basic plot of *A Trip to Calais* is retained in *The Capuchin*, although some characters (Luke Lapelle and Gregory Gingham) are omitted and some (Viper and Sir Harry Hamper) are added. As in *A Trip to Calais*, Dick and Jenny arrive in France, pursued by the Minnikins, and Jenny takes refuge in the convent. Viper, who is tutor and traveling companion to Sir Harry Hamper, a tea merchant formerly the Minnikins' neighbor, has used his position to fleece thoroughly his employer, and in this respect differs little from Foote's other cozeners. But Viper does not stop at preying on credulous old men with more money than wit. He devises a scheme to lure Jenny from the convent, with the intention of having Sir Harry seduce her. Seeing Jenny, however, Viper decides that she is too young and pretty for an old man; he offers her his protection as a clergyman, and then attempts rape.

Foote's Dr. Viper is a collection of unpleasant attributes rather than a fully realized character. Sir Harry Hamper on the other hand is a truly comic creation. He inherits Luke Lapelle's mangled French from the earlier play, along with Luke's willingness to buy the flattery of servants. Sir Harry, once a tradesman, is an old bachelor who recently has come into a title. To gain the approval of his young mistress in London he has made the grand tour, scouring off all the "sneaking snivelling cit" (107), as he supposes. His tour, under Viper's tutelage, has been a lesson in profligacy, though his chief pleasure lies not in the actual gaming and whoring but in being thought a fashionable rake. He therefore is willing to debauch Jenny, especially if it will be reported in the London press. And Viper advises that "I think it will be right, at your time of life, to report it a rape; it will do your vivacity and vigour a good deal of credit" (98). Sir Harry combines the credulous cit and mindless adulation for French customs in a delightfully silly variation on the theme of "no fool like an old fool".

Except for Harry Hamper, then, *The Capuchin* is inferior to *A Trip to Calais,* partly because Viper is an unsatisfactory character. His attempted rape of Jenny distorts the shape of the play. Her screams summon the entire *dramatis personae,* including the Colonel, a survival from the original play, implausibly introduced here to give assurance that Viper's exploits will be reported to the Calais police. The ending is sentimentalized and perfunctory. Mr. and Mrs. Minnikin accept their daughter's choice of Dicky Drugget, a denouement less satisfactory than the original ironically appropriate solution in which the rebellious girl willingly enters Lady Kitty's service. In the final analysis it is the absence of that coarse, aging, titled harridan that deprives *The Capuchin* of vitality.

Discussion of *A Trip to Calais* and *The Capuchin* has necessarily involved an excursion into biography. Foote saw life as material for his drama and did not scruple to depict living persons. In *A Trip to Calais,* however, his dramatic art precipitated events even more sensational than those he portrayed on the stage. The Duchess of Kingston's trial for bigamy which finally took place in April, 1776, and Foote's trial for sodomy in December of the same year stand in relation to these plays as cause and effect. Emotions aroused by such events require expression in drama more serious than Foote was capable of, along with an imagination which could transform these highly personal quarrels into a conflict of general interest. Perhaps it is the unrealized potential of his subject matter that makes his pale revenge on Jackson in *The Capuchin* seem spiteful, petty, and essentially inadequate.

The Capuchin was Foote's last play. The sale of his interest in the Haymarket Theatre to George Colman the Elder was completed on January 16, 1777, just under a month after Foote's harrowing trial and subsequent collapse. In accordance with the terms of the sale, Foote acted for Colman at the Haymarket during the summer of 1777, but was on three occasions stricken with convulsive seizures. After recuperating at Brighton, Foote returned to London late in September preparatory to spending the winter in France. He got only as far as Dover, where a sudden violent attack of convulsions proved fatal.[21] At the very least, Jackson's libels had created stress which increased Foote's vulnerability to physical illness.

CHAPTER 11

Satire as Literary Criticism

I *Grub Street Satirized*

LIKE many literary figures of the eighteenth century, Foote satirized the booksellers and the hack writers of Grub Street, and deprecated the debased public taste which supported them. In *The Author, The Bankrupt,* and *The Capuchin* he attacked scandalmongering newspapers and the abuses of literary patronage. In *The Patron* he ridiculed the stupidity of an aristocratic author too cowardly to admit authorship of his play, which has been damned at the theater. Foote habitually directed jibes at foolish playwrights. One of the wittiest is recounted by Cooke: "A foreigner being present at a musical piece which was damned the first night of its performance, asked Foote who the author was. Being told that his name was *St. John,* he asked again, '*St. Jean, St. Jean, quel St. Jean?*' (St. John, St. John, what St. John?')—'*Oh, Monsieur!*' cried Foote; '*le gentilhomme sans la tête.* (Oh, Sir! the gentleman without a head).' "[1]

II Tragedy-a-la-Mode

Two types of drama which lent themselves to parody were burlesqued by Foote in brief interludes or playlets. *Tragedy-a-la-Mode,* or *Modern Tragedy* (1761), based on William Whitehead's *Fatal Constancy,*[2] is a parody of the heroic tragedy popular during the Restoration and early eighteenth century. In *Tragedy-a-la-Mode* Foote employs the rehearsal form, with Manly and Townly the critics present at the first trial of Fustian's play, *Love till Death.* The hero, Golcondus, and the heroine, Lindamira, are given multisyllabic romantic names typical of heroic tragedy. Fustian's desire for novelty and economy, however, results in a startling innovation. Only Golcondus is played by an actor; the other characters, who

130

have no speaking parts, are portrayed by puppets, or pasteboard figures, who undoubtedly are a reflection on the thinness of heroic-play characterization. The play itself is written in blank verse which exaggerates the heightened emotions and operatic language of heroic tragedy. Bathos is utilized to comic effect, as when Golcondus begs Lindamira to flee with him:

> And wilt thou seek with me some happier shore,
> Where fathers, mothers, friends we'll meet no
>   more.
> The merchant thus at home a bankrupt made,
> Seeks out another clime and drives another trade.[3]

Much of the humor in the play, however, arises from the incongruous echoes of Shakespeare. In act 1, Golcondus speaks like Othello: "Stars fall from heav'n, suns forget to rise,/ And Chaos come, when Lindamira dies."[4] At the end of the play, Golcondus, stabbing first the king and then himself, dies with this plea to his friend Tribus:

> Tribus, I charge thee live.
> Oh! if humanity can touch thy breast,
> Entomb'd with Lindamira let me rest;
> Tell my sad tale, that all the world may weep,
> I'm very sick—One kiss, good night, I'm fast asleep.[5]

Other echoes of *Hamlet* and *Othello* add to the ridiculousness of *Love till Death*.

In *The Wandering Patentee*, Tate Wilkinson, who had played Golcondus to Foote's Fustian, discusses the reception of *Tragedy a-la-Mode*: "When this piece was first acted by Mr. Foote, with PASTEBOARD FIGURES, it entirely failed in the effect; but with PERFORMERS, *accoutred ridiculously pompous* and in *fierce whiskered high tragedy*, the effect those dumb actors had assisted my Imitations, and received unbounded applause."[6] The utilization of actors to portray puppets is in itself a criticism of the stilted and unrealistic behavior of the characters in many heroic tragedies. The satire also strikes at another of heroic tragedy's vulnerable points: its "prostitution of the excellence [of theatrical grief]" against which Foote had years earlier cautioned the actor Barry.

III   Piety in Pattens

Foote's use of satire as a mode of literary criticism is again exemplified in his burlesque of another dramatic form which flourished
in the eighteenth century, the sentimental comedy. *Piety in Pattens,*
or *The Handsome Housemaid,* first performed in 1773, is an antisentimental interlude parodying Bickerstaffe's comic opera *The
Maid of the Mill* and Richardson's *Pamela.* The playlet formed part
of Foote's *Primitive Puppet Show.* For two hundred years *Piety in
Pattens* existed only in manuscript form. Recently, an excellent
critical edition by Samuel N. Bogorad and the late Robert Gale
Noyes has appeared. My references are to Bogorad's text.

Foote introduced this entertainment with an exordium which
took the form of a satirical address on puppetry, filled with humorous
allusions to contemporary opera, drama, and acting. The huge crowd
which filled the Haymarket was displeased with the performance,
perhaps because those in the galleries could not properly see the
puppets,[8] though contemporary reviews also suggest that the gallery
had expected something resembling a Punch and Judy show.[9] The
possibility that the uproar and rioting which broke out after the
performance was the work of a faction organized to prevent Foote
mimicking other actors, particularly Garrick, is also advanced in
some reports of the first night. In any case the entertainment was
too short and Foote expanded it, adding a humorous dialogue with
Punch, presumably as a sop to the gallery. The revised version was
better understood and more warmly received, according to the
account in the *General Evening Post* for March 6–9, 1773:

The audience tasted the salt of the satire, they saw the evident intention
of the burlesque upon modern comedy; they confessed that a dull truth,
when stripp'd of the artificial guise of words, was the essence of the gen-
erality of those sentiments the writers of the present age lard their pieces
with, and convinced of having adopted a false taste, they joined in their
own verdict, by loudly approving what may justly be termed *Foote's Mirror
for sentimental Writers.*[10]

Piety in Pattens was later acted as an interlude with live actors
instead of puppets, and in this form Foote's satire on sentimental
comedy—just as pointed but more amusing—produced hearty
laughter in the audience.

The plot of *Piety in Pattens* features only four characters: Squire

Turniptop and his three servants: Mrs. Candy the housekeeper, Polly Pattens the handsome housemaid, and Thomas the butler. Polly is tempted by the Squire's offer to take her to London as his mistress, but Thomas' moral advice persuades her to leave Turniptop's house in order to preserve her honor. The Squire, impressed with Polly's virtue, offers to marry her, but Polly refuses, claiming that as Thomas has saved her from shame he should have her hand. Noble sentiment reaches epidemic proportions when Thomas refuses her: "No, no, Polly, no. what, shall Thomas that loves you dearer than Life, stand in the Gap & stop your Preferment? never, never. you desarve the Squire for presarving your Vartue, & he desarves you by knowing how to reward it. be happy together" (34–35). Not to be outdone, Polly refuses both suitors: "There is one part still to be acted by me. let Polly Pattens shew the World how truly delicate a House Maid can be. as your Passion, Sir, & Thomas's are equal, I cannot purfur one without afflicting the other. Justice & Gratitude therefore demand as I must not have both, to take— neither" (35). The play concludes with a return from the artificiality and false delicacy of sentimental comedy to the realm of common sense:

Sq[uire]. But rouse thee, Squire, shake off this lazy Passion, be thyself
  From the deluded Syren's charms, I'll fly
  And Guns, Hounds, Horses shall her loss supply.
[*Thomas.*] To washing Bottles I, and fitting Corks
  Brushing my Plate and cleaning Knives and Forks.
Po[lly]. Welcome again my favorite Mops and Brooms
  To making Beds I go, and sweeping Rooms.
Sq[uire]. By different Duties when the mind's possest
  Love finds no Entrance in the human breast.
All. No Entrance in the human breast. (50–51)

The bathetic mock-sentimentality of the finale is quite in accord with Foote's address to the audience, as reported by Genest:

Foote informed the audience that the piece about to be performed was a Sentimental Comedy called "the Handsome Housemaid, or Piety in Pattens"—that they would not discover much wit or humour in it, for his brother writers had all agreed that it was highly improper, and beneath the dignity of a mixed assembly, to show any signs of joyful satisfaction; and that creating a laugh was forcing the higher order of an audience to a vulgar and mean use of their muscles—he had therefore, like them, given up the sensual for the sentimental style.[11]

In *Satire and Panegyric in the Plays of Samuel Foote*, R. V. Wharton has noted that Foote's *Piety in Pattens* ridicules "several of the stock characteristics of sentimental comedy; the abysmal ignorance of the sentimental heroine; the alliance between prurience and sentimentalism; the black-and-white cast of character; the oceans of tears; the sententious platitudes." Wharton feels that the attack "centres on the naive conviction of the sentimentalist that the most powerfully selfish impulses may be easily overcome."[12] It is easy to grant Wharton's first point, that Foote satirizes the stock characteristics of sentimental comedy. The scene where Thomas gives his wordy advice to the ignorant housemaid exemplifies several of these characteristics, and is in many ways the highlight of the play:

Thomas. The Squire, I see, is bent on your Ruin.
Polly. No, No, Thomas, the Squire loves me too well.
Thomas. You? it is himself that he loves, & wants to gratify that partial Affection by the Possession of you. he loves you from the Love of himself: only think, Polly, to be robb'd of your Innocence?
Polly. My Innocence?
[Thomas]. Ay, Child, for whatever the Squire & Men of his Turn may tell you—believe this as a Truth—the Woman who loses her Virtue, from that very Instant all her Chastity's gone.
Polly. Is it possible?
[Thomas]. True. & like the Stream that descends from the Mountains, will never return to its Source.
Polly. These are Wonders, Thomas, you tell me, but how should a poor ignorant Girl be able to find out such Things?
[Thomas]. And as to such Sparks as my Master, they are no sooner gratify'd, than they are satisfy'd.
Polly. Amazing!
[Thomas]. & when they desert you, Polly, then you are forsaken.
Polly. Wonderful.
[Thomas]. & being left to Want, you fall into a State of Distress.
Polly. Miserable Creature!
[Thomas]. Till at last being worn out with Care, when your last Breath departs from your Lips.
Polly. What then?
[Thomas]. Then Polly you are dead. (28–30)

Thomas's tautological advice and Polly's brief phrases make the entire scene almost an operatic duet. The sequence is skillfully orchestrated; the question and answer technique, the pauses for emphasis indicated in Thomas's carefully phrased speeches, and the falling cadence of "Then Polly you are dead" combine to accentuate the emotional overtones of Polly's situation. Thomas's rhetorical redundancy, amusing enough in itself, is used by Foote for a masterly prolonging and drawing out of "feeling" in imitation of the sentimental style. Later, Polly proclaims the value of Thomas's counsel:

> Would every Chambermaid forsake her Pride,
> & take an honest Butler for her Guide,
> Them of their Vartue, Squires ne'er could cheat,
> Nor with lewd Misses people every Street. (30)

Only qualified agreement, however, can be given to Wharton's claim that Foote's attack is focused upon the sentimentalist's unrealistic belief in the easy triumph of personal virtue over selfish impulses. The noble effusions and improbable fifth-act reformations of sentimental comedy which Foote mocks in his playlet lend themselves to parody because, as Wharton implies, they are essentially unrealistic and idealized representations of human behavior. Characters that behave in this manner are wooden, and this is surely one of Foote's chief targets. He reveals the lifelessness of sentimental comedy by refusing to furnish his interlude with the vivid characters for which his other plays are noted. *Piety in Pattens* contains an implicit criticism of the sentimentalists' view of human nature, and an explicit demonstration that Foote found sentimental drama boring and empty.

IV   *Foote's Attack on Sentimentalism*

Discussion of *Piety in Pattens* leads almost inevitably to an evaluation of the extent of Foote's attack on sentimentalism. Although Goldsmith and Sheridan are universally credited with initiating the move to oust sentimental comedy and reinstate a comedy of manners directly descended from Congreve and Etherege, *Piety in Pattens* was performed at the Haymarket on February 15, 1773, one full

month before Goldsmith's *She Stoops to Conquer*, making Foote
a pioneer in antisentimental drama. One reviewer claimed that
Foote's burlesque was in part responsible for the success of Goldsmith's comedy: "Notwithstanding the innate merit of Dr. Goldsmith's new piece, it is not to be doubted, but that the ridicule
aimed by Foote, at what has for some time past been received as
comedy by the town, aided in establishing the play, called, *She
Stoops to Conquer*."[13] In his discussion of *Piety in Pattens*, Ernest
Bernbaum makes the following observation: "Foote . . . had a
larger comprehension of the nature of the genre than any of its
other antagonists since Vanbrugh. Most of the attacks upon it, both
before Foote's time and thereafter, were directed against its sententious style and serious tone. Foote struck deeper, and made
ridiculous the sentimental desire to idealize common life."[14] Furthermore, there is evidence in the lists of plays performed that even
at the height of the sentimental vogue, various forms of laughing
comedy flourished as afterpiece drama. Foote's comedies are def-
initely in this afterpiece tradition; his prolific output can thus be
considered as in part counteracting the trend toward sentimentality.

It has been alleged, however, that many of his plays show pronounced sentimental tendencies. That certain of Foote's plays in-
volve situations also common to sentimental comedy is undeniable.
The Englishman in Paris, The Minor, The Nabob, and *The Bankrupt*
are cases in point. But, as Belden points out, "Foote is less eager
than the Sentimentalists to inculcate ethical notions, [and] he is,
on the other hand, less satisfied with shallow and formal adjustments
of moral situations."[15] Most of Foote's rogues and predators are
successful, unrepentant, and unpunished. His commitment to realistic portrayal of character precluded the improbable reformations
and self-sacrifice of sentimental comedy. Furthermore, the criteria
applied in discussing the sentimental aspects of *The Minor* in chapter 5 apply equally to Foote's other comedies, with the natural
exception of *Piety in Pattens*. It is not the presence of sentimental
situations alone, but the prolonging of them which distinguishes
sentimental comedy, and in none of his plays does Foote allow even
his most hapless characters to linger long over their misfortunes.
The rapid succession of incidents and humorous characters prevents
such concentration upon the emotional aspects of the plays. By
contrast *Piety in Pattens*, although admittedly brief, deals with but
one topic: Polly's "vartue." If Foote was influenced by the senti-

mentalists in any major way, it may be in the fact that his wit is generally free of sexual innuendo.

Foote's use of puppets or of puppetlike actors in *Piety in Pattens* and *Tragedy a-la-Mode* goes beyond satirical criticism of the sentimental comedy and the heroic tragedy. Fustian, in *Tragedy*, sees puppetry in a wider perspective: "Reflect only on how many puppets you meet in the world: For who ever acts not upon his own principles, but condescends to receive direction and motion from another, is to all intents and purposes, though composed of flesh and blood, as arrant a puppet as mine of wood and wire."[16] The implication is that not only actors but most of mankind may be mere puppets. In the same play, Foote hits at the lionizing of certain actors by the audiences:

> It is not the play, but the player; not the exploits of a Richard or a Tamerlane, but the fame of his representative that the people come to see. If then we can get rid of all the supernumerary personages, and the whole business of the scene into one mouth, we can ease the poet's labour, lessen the manager's expence, and save our own time, and produce the favourite actor.[17]

The interlude, which begins with an exchange between Project and the Prompter satirizing the feigned illnesses and all too real pregnancies of certain leading actresses, thus incorporates satire on the players, criticism of heroic tragedy, and a thrust at the puppetlike condition of supposed human beings.

Foote did not attempt to write tragedy, nor did he ever produce a comedy which could without reservation be called sentimental. In *Tragedy a-la-Mode* and *Piety in Pattens*, his parodies of heroic tragedy and sentimental comedy, Foote used puppets as a visual comment on the lack of realism in the dramatic forms he satirized— clear evidence of his distaste for both.

Similarities in subject matter and in treatment place Foote's satirical literary criticism in the tradition of the theatrical burlesques produced in the 1730s by Henry Fielding. Both playwrights adopted the format of Buckingham's *Rehearsal*, and both utilized puppets in certain of their dramatic satires. *Tom Thumb* and *Pasquin* burlesque the excesses of heroic tragedy, which Foote later attacked in *Tragedy a-la-Mode*. In *The Author's Farce*, Fielding, using a puppet show and the familiar rehearsal device, satirized Grub Street as well as the mediocrity of the early eighteenth-century stage, just as Foote was to do a few years later in *The Author*. Foote did not incorporate into his works the political satire for which Fielding was noted, but he and Fielding had much the same flair for personal satire, and their plays reflect many of the same interests.

CHAPTER 12

The Mask of Infinite Pleasantry

I *Pictures of Vice and Folly*

FOOTE boasted to Boswell that he had given sixteen new characters to English comedy.[1] His boast was justified; the creation of comic characters was one of his strengths, as the anonymous author of *Wit for the Ton* noted soon after the playwright's death in 1777:

> His *fort* was the exhibition of character, in which . . . for boldness of outline, and strength and truth of colouring, he stood unrivalled. His dialogue in general is terse, easy, and witty. His scenes teem with true humour; and under the mask of infinite pleasantry, convey the strongest satire. No dramatic writer ever paid less attention to the fables of his plays; and yet there are not to be seen, in the whole round of modern pieces, so many striking pictures of vice and folly as have been drawn by the late Mr. Foote.(7)

Correspondingly, it was to character that he assigned primary importance when he theorized about comedy in *The Roman and English Comedy Consider'd and Compar'd,* and later in the preface to *The Comic Theatre.* Those characters that impress the reader are Foote's vividly drawn eccentrics, such as Sir Gregory Gazette, Sir Penurious Trifle, Mrs. Cole, Sam Shift, Major Sturgeon, Jerry Sneak, Zachary Fungus, Solomon Flint, Sir Christopher Cripple, and Sir Matthew Mite. They are firmly in the humours tradition; each acts according to his bias. This too is in accord with Foote's dramatic theory, propounded before he had really begun his career as a playwright. Like humours characters in general, Foote's memorable creations are to be laughed at, rather than laughed with. No sympathy is possible, or invited, for characters drawn in this manner.

An examination of the *dramatis personae* listed for premiere performances reveals that in many cases Foote played two or three characters in the same comedy, and these were invariably the unforgettable eccentrics and predators, rather than the somewhat bland, almost interchangeable, English peers and merchants who served as heroes in his plays. The dichotomy between these very ordinary characters and Foote's colorful caricatures, which seems to indicate unevenness in characterization, is also consonant with Foote's critical theories. The two types of character correspond to his distinction, in *The Roman and English Comedy,* between Men of Humor and Humorists. Recognizing the comic potential of the humorists in his society, Foote recreated them on his stage. His insistence upon "unity of character" is borne out in these unregenerate eccentrics. It is no accident that Foote himself played many of the unrepentant villains in his plays, for they share with their creator that combination of brazenness and resourcefulness which enables them to capitalize on the most unpromising situations— perhaps, like Foote, to earn ten pounds on the strength of an uncle's notoriety as a murderer.

Foote's versatility as an actor is amplified in his dramatic writings. The ear for characteristic idiom which made him a great mimic also gave him the ability to vary the language spoken by his characters. This was one of the aspects of his work praised by his first biographer, Cooke, by no means an uncritical admirer of Foote: "His dialogue shows a solid and extensive *knowledge of mankind* in their various customs and manners; now exhibiting the keenest strokes of temporary satire, and now a flow of humour which nothing but the closest judgment, and the most penetrating discernment of human nature, could suggest."[2] Foote's comedies demand a keen ear of the reader. Few critics aside from Foote's contemporaries, who had the advantage of seeing the plays, have recognized the extent of his mastery of dialogue, and of language in general. A notable exception is Bogorad, who points out in his introduction to *Piety in Pattens* that Foote's literary style has been underrated. "He was always tremendously interested in the study of speech: its oddities, idioms, reiterations, and unfinished sentences. The dialogue of his plays, with its frequent emphasis on colloquialism and idiomatic expression, apparently strives to reflect the conversation of his age."[3] Cooke called him "the truest *conversation copy* of the times in which he wrote."[4] Each of Foote's humorists reflects in his speech his particular preoccupation or specialization. The dialect too is suited to the speaker, and to his position in society. *The Maid of Bath* affords several examples of this excellence. Flint, the miser, places his trust in his money, and in the law:

Money! I know its worth, and therefore can't too carefully keep it: At this very instant I have a proof of its value; it enables me to laugh at that squeamish impertinent girl, and despise the weak efforts of your impotent malice: Call me forth to your courts when you please; that will procure me able defenders, and good witnesses too, if they are wanted. (54)

Family pride and meanness are mingled in an earlier speech describing his house:

I have boarded up most of the windows, in order to save paying the tax. But to my thinking, our bed-chamber, Miss, is the most pleasantest place in the house . . . there is a large bow-window facing the East, that does fine for drying of herbs: It is hung around with hatchments of all the folks that have died in the family; and then the pigeon-house is over our heads. (32)

Billy Button describes Solomon Flint and Kitty Linnet in tailor's idiom:

Why, to be sure, his honour is a little stricken in years, as a body may say; and, take all the care that one can, time will wear the nap from even superfine cloth; stitches tear, and elbows will out, as they say— . . . But she is a tight bit of stuff, and I am confident will turn out well in the wearing. I once had some thoughts myself of taking measure of Miss. (19)

The little tailor's scorn for Flint's offer of Kitty's hand is again couched in the words of his trade: "He was out in his man! let him give his cast cloaths to his coachman; Billy Button can afford a new suit of his own" (55). Such aspects of language are, in effect, the stuff that characters are made of. This also Foote had paid heed to in his early dramatic criticism, insisting on "unity of dialogue" as the first requirement for comedy, and as the basis of the humours character. Those who cavil at the agreement between theory and practice in Foote's work tend to derogate his dramatic criticism as mere apologetics, produced in defense of such controversial plays as *The Minor*. His critical principles, however, were formulated in the same year that his first play appeared at the Haymarket. Foote must be given credit for consistency, and for practicing what he preached, rather than criticized for preaching what he practiced.

Foote's strength as a master of situation is demonstrated in nearly all his plays. In the creation of comic incidents which reveal the humorous peculiarities of his characters, Foote was both inventive and original. It is evident also that his mastery of situation and his skill in choosing a style of conversation appropriate to the speaker are subservient to his avowed purpose in comedy, the creation of character. The quality of Foote's comic gift is surprisingly modern, akin to the zany, near-surrealist humor of satirical revue. His extravagant wit often ignores the demands of plot, though in discussing Foote's apparent indifference to conventional plot and structure, it is well to remember that the form of his plays was unavoidably shaped by his habitual doubling and tripling of parts.

Certain weaknesses are often attributed to Foote as a dramatist. Inability to delineate emotion, sketchy plot development, and a heavy reliance upon mimicry of individuals are among the most frequently voiced criticisms. While these would be crippling faults in a romantic comedy, or even a comedy of manners, they are not necessarily flaws in Foote's satiric comedy. His intentions dictated the form of his plays. He chose to delineate the faults and affectations of his society, and these faults he exemplified in his humours characters. If the portrait often relied heavily upon imitation, the follies and vices Foote mocked were characteristic of his period in history. H. B. Baker pays this tribute to the comprehensiveness of Foote's satire: "To those who would form a perfect conception of the manners of . . . [Foote's age], his works are invaluable; there is not a folly, a vice, a sham of the time, which they do not expose."[5] The caricatures of individuals which delighted or incensed Samuel Foote's contemporaries are largely lost on the modern reader, who perhaps, therefore, finds it easier to recognize the delineation of the type, which underlies most of Foote's satiric characterizations.

II *Influence and Reputation*

Foote's comedies did not, with a few exceptions, long outlive their author. They are essentially vehicles for an actor with a flair for mimicry and caricature who can bring to life Foote's satirical portraits. An appreciation of the topical allusions in the plays is dependent upon a basic knowledge of the eighteenth-century social and political background, though the situations and the eccentricities of behavior Foote depicts are universal. However, changing standards of taste and decorum in the nineteenth century militated against topical satire. Foote's commitment to Old Comedy attracted no followers, though later dramatists like Goldsmith, Sheridan, and Thomas Holcroft[6] borrowed freely from his works.

Because his plays are not performed, Foote's reputation now depends solely on their value as literature, which tends to neglect such considerations as theatrical effectiveness. As previously mentioned, his literary style has been underrated. Now that his plays have been reprinted, it is to be hoped that interest in them will revive. There is a need for critical editions which would place his works in the social context of eighteenth-century London. These would make his humor more universally accessible, and do much to rescue him from comparative, and undeserved, obscurity.

III *The Achievement*

As a writer of dramatic satires, Foote earned a significant place in theater history. His talent, which drew upon the many facets of his irrepressible nature, brought audiences to the Haymarket for thirty years. A leading exemplar of the satiric afterpiece tradition, he not only wrote more than twenty comedies, but produced and acted in most of them himself. As George Colman, his contemporary fellow dramatist and sometime rival, noted: "There is no Shakespeare or Roscius upon record who, like Foote, supported a theatre for a series of years by his own acting, in his own writings;—and for ten years of that time, upon a wooden leg!"[7] It is fitting that Colman's assessment should be of the man as well as the dramatist, for even at a distance of two hundred years the fascination of Samuel Foote, the wit and raconteur, remains strong—an author inseparable from his works, which reflect both his extraordinary personality and the manners, follies, and vices of his time.

Notes and References

Chapter One

1. John Wells Wilkinson, "The Life and Works of Samuel Foote" (typescript, 1936), I, 127 notes the common error of citing Foote's year of birth as 1720, and includes a photograph of the register of St. Mary, Truro, Cornwall, showing the entry "Samuel Son to Samuel ffoote Esqr. & Eleanor his Wife baptised January 27." On the same page, headed 1720, a line is drawn after the entry for March 5 and 1721 printed, firmly establishing Foote's birth in 1721 (new style).

2. William Cooke, *Memoirs of Samuel Foote*, 3 vols. (London, 1805), I, 18.

3. Ibid., II, 34. Cooke notes that Foote was given ten pounds, with the promise of a further ten if sales reached a given point.

4. James Boswell, *Boswell's Life of Johnson*, ed. George Birkbeck Hill, rev. L. F. Powell, 6 vols. (Oxford, 1964), V, 37.

5. Cooke, *Memoirs*, I, 13.

6. *Memoirs*, II, 3–4.

7. "On the Comic Writers of England, No. 12—Foote and the Farce-Writers," n.s. 8 (1872), 305.

8. *Boswell's Life of Johnson*, V, 391.

9. Mary Megie Belden, *The Dramatic Work of Samuel Foote* (1929; reprint ed., New York, 1970), p. 2.

10. J. W. Wilkinson, I, 180. The anecdotes are in Cooke, *Memoirs*, III, 61–64.

11. *The London Stage: 1660–1800, Part 3, 1729–1747*, ed. Arthur H. Scouten, 2 vols. (Carbondale, Illinois, 1961), I, xlviii–li. Further references to this work will be designated "Scouten," with the appropriate page and volume noted.

12. Ibid., p. liii.

13. *The London Stage: 1660–1800, Part 4, 1747–1776*, ed. George Winchester Stone, Jr., 3 vols. (Carbondale, Illinois, 1962), I, xxiv. Further references to this work will be designated "Stone," with the appropriate page and volume noted.

14. Scouten, I, liv.

15. *Memoirs*, I, 42–43.

16. John Genest, ed., *Some Account of the English Stage*, 10 vols. (Bath, 1832), IV, 20–21.

17. Ibid., V, 529.

18. Leo Hughes, *The Drama's Patrons: A Study of the Eighteenth-Century London Audience* (Austin, Texas, 1971), pp. 181–83. Hughes considers 1800 a maximum capacity for Drury Lane after the alterations in 1747 and 1762.

19. Scouten, I, lviii–lix.

20. Ibid., p. ciii–civ.

21. Tate Wilkinson, *Memoirs of His Own Life*, 4 vols. (York, 1790), I. 24.

22. William Cooke, in *Theatrical Biography*, 2 vols. (London, 1772), II, 114.

23. Genest, IV, 225–26.

24. Scouten, I, clvii.

25. Genest, IV, 226.

26. James J. Lynch, *Box, Pit, and Gallery: Stage and Society in Johnson's London* (Berkeley, 1953), p. 11.

27. *Memoirs*, II, 103.

28. Stone, I, lxx.

29. Ibid., pp. clxxiv–clxxv.

30. (Harmondsworth, Middlesex, 1962), pp. 15–16.

Chapter Two

1. The second act of *Diversions* is printed in Cooke, *Memoirs*, III, 113–29. *Tragedy a-la-Mode* is printed in Tate Wilkinson, *The Wandering Patentee*, 4 vols. (York, 1795), I, 285–99.

2. Belden, p. 53.

3. *Philological Quarterly*, 45 (January, 1966), 191–208.

4. *The Jacobite's Journal*, no. 22 (April 30, 1748).

5. George Anne Bellamy, *Apology for the Life of George Anne Bellamy* (London, 1785), II, 205-11, quoted in Belden, pp. 72–73.

6. Stone, III, 1989–92.

7. Cooke, *Memoirs*, III, 113.

8. Ibid., p. 121.

9. Wallace Cable Brown, *Charles Churchill: Poet, Rake, and Rebel* (Lawrence, Kansas, 1953), pp. 48–49. See also Edward H. Weatherly, "Foote's Revenge on Churchill and Lloyd," *Huntington Library Quarterly*, 9 (1945), 49–60.

10. Belden, p. 168.

11. Genest, *Some Account of the English Stage*, IV, 599

12. Belden, p. 168.

13. 1747; reprint ed., New York, 1971), p. 31.

14. Leo Hughes, *A Century of English Farce* (Princeton, 1956), pp. 4–9.

15. Ibid., p. 13. Hughes quotes Blount's *Glossographia* (1661).

16. (London, 1970), p. x.

17. *Of Dramatic Poesy and Other Critical Essays*, I, 146.

18. Samuel A. Golden, "An Early Defense of Farce," in *Studies in Honor of John Wilcox,* ed. A. Dayle Wallace and Woodburn O. Ross (Detroit, 1958). pp. 65–66.

19. Hughes, *A Century of English Farce,* p. 16.

20. *Bon Mots of Samuel Foote and Theodore Hooke,* ed. Walter Jerrold, with grotesques by Aubrey Beardsley (London, 1894), p. 114.

21. *Boswell's Life of Johnson,* II, 95.

22. 1 (June, 1765), 280.

23. "A Letter from Mr. Foote to the Reverend Author of the 'Remarks, Critical and Christian,' on the Minor," (printed in Cooke, *Memoirs,* III, 160–201, 163.

24. Willard Connely, *Laurence Sterne as Yorick* (London, 1958), p. 155.

25. Ibid., p. 14.

26. *The Comic Theatre,* I, vii.

27. Bevis, ed., *Eighteenth Century Drama: Afterpieces,* pp. 243–44.

28. Ibid., p. x.

Chapter Three

1. *The Dramatic Works of Samuel Foote,* 2 vols. (1809; reprint ed., London, 1968), I, 3. Unless otherwise indicated, all subsequent references to Foote's plays are from this edition. Pagination is not consecutive; therefore, page references are to the play specified.

2. Stone, I, 108–29.

3. 5 vols. (London, 1762), I, v.

4. Ibid., p. viii.

5. Ibid., p. vi.

6. Simon Trefman, *Sam. Foote, Comedian, 1720–1777* (New York, 1971), p. 51.

7. Stone, I, 284–85, 287.

8. See Moira Dearnley, *The Poetry of Christopher Smart* (London, 1969), pp. 22–24.

9. Cooke, *Memoirs,* I, 137.

10. Ibid.

Chapter Four

1. Stone, I, 360.

2. Trefman, pp. 61, 64, n. 70 quotes from Foote's letter to John Delaval dated April 5, 1753 (Folger Shakespeare Library, MS, W.b. 472).

3. Ibid., pp. 73–80. Foote's version opened on February 3, 1756, at Covent Garden; Murphy's on April 3, 1756, at Drury Lane. Trefman discusses in detail both Murphy's *Englishman Return'd* and his satire on Foote in an unperformed two act play, *The Spouter; or, The Triple Revenge*, published just before the production of Foote's *Englishman Return'd*. See also Simon Trefman, "Arthur Murphy's Long Lost *Englishman from Paris:* A Manuscript Discovered," *Theatre Notebook*, 20 (Summer, 1966), 137–41.

4. Genest, *Some Account of the English Stage*, IV, 467. See also "The Life of Samuel Foote," *Dramatic Works of Samuel Foote* (1809) I, 11.

5. In George Paston (pseud. Emily Morse Symonds), *Social Caricature in the Eighteenth Century* (London, 1905), plate 67, foll. p. 48.

6. *Town and Country Magazine*, 9 (Nov. 1777), 599–600.

7. Thomas Davies, *Memoirs of the Life of David Garrick* (London, 1780), I, 193.

8. Ibid., 201.

9. Trefman, pp. 103–4, n. 7. John Delaval was Francis Blake Delaval's brother.

10. Davies, I, 194.

Chapter Five

1. Trefman, pp. 100–103.

2. Belden, p. 85.

3. Prior to leaving for Dublin the previous November, Foote had read portions of his play as part of his *Comic Lectures* (Stone, II, 755).

4. Ibid., pp. 801–5, 823–26.

5. Belden, p. 81.

6. See for example Belden, p. 191; Percy Fitzgerald, *Samuel Foote, A Biography* (London, 1910), p. 192; John Forster, "Samuel Foote," in *Historical and Biographical Essays* (London, 1858), II, 377.

7. Belden, p. 82.

8. See for example, Belden, p. 175, and Robert Verner Wharton, "Satire and Panegyric in the Plays of Samuel Foote," (Ph.D. diss., Columbia University, 1954), pp. 131–32.

9. *English Sentimental Drama* (East Lansing, Michigan, 1957), pp. 32–35.

10. Forster, "Samuel Foote," p. 379.

11. "A Letter . . . to the Reverend Author of the 'Remarks . . .' on the Minor," in Cooke, *Memoirs*, III, 175–76.

12. Jonathan Swift, "Verses on the Death of Dr. Swift," lines 520–21.

13. Forster, "Samuel Foote," p. 371.

14. Belden, pp. 85–106.

15. Forster, "Samuel Foote," p. 373.

16. Ibid., p. 374.

17. Ibid., p. 370. Forster's estimates are surely exaggerated, but his suggestion that Whitefield could attract such vast numbers implies the establishment's fear of Methodism.

18. Ibid., p. 371.

19. J. H. Plumb, *England in the Eighteenth Century* (Harmondsworth, Middlesex, 1966), pp. 93–95.

20. Forster, "Samuel Foote," pp. 369–70.

21. Trefman, appendix, pp. 271–82.

22. Stone, I, cliii.

Chapter Six

1. Prologue to *The Lyar*, p. 3.

2. Belden, p. 189.

3. Shirley Strum Kenny, ed., *The Plays of Richard Steele* (Oxford, 1971), p. 107.

4. Cooke, *Memoirs*, II, 55.

5. Belden, p. 188.

6. Ibid., p. 189.

7. Cooke, *Memoirs*, I, 119. See also Trefman, p. 121.

8. *Boswell's Life of Johnson*, II, 434.

9. Trefman, p. 123.

10. Quoted in Stone, II, 934.

11. George Taylor, " 'The Just Delineation of the Passions': Theories of Acting in the Age of Garrick," in *Essays on The Eighteenth-Century English Stage,* ed. Kenneth Richards and Peter Thomson (London, 1972), p. 53.

12. *Samuel Foote's Primitive Puppet-Shew Featuring Piety in Pattens: A Critical Edition,* ed. Samuel N. Bogorad and Robert Gale Noyes, *Theatre Survey,* 14, no 1a (Fall, 1973), 4. In further references this play is designated as *Piety in Pattens,* ed. Bogorad.

13. Trefman, p. 123.

14. Christopher Hibbert, *The Personal History of Samuel Johnson* (London, 1971), p. 125.

15. *The Minor*, p. 36.

16. Cooke, *Memoirs*, III, 137.

17. Forster, "Samuel Foote," p. 400.

18. William W. Appleton, *Charles Macklin: An Actor's Life* (Cambridge, Mass., 1961), pp. 100–101.

19. Trefman, p. 126.

20. Appleton, p. 100.

21. Trefman, pp. 125–26.

22. Stone, II, 996.

23. Cooke, *Memoirs*, III, 130–31.

24. Ibid., p. 132.
25. Ibid., p. 130.
26. Ibid., p. 139.
27. Ibid., pp. 139–41. This address also appeared in *The Public Advertiser*, January 28, 1763.
28. Belden, p. 113.

Chapter Seven

1. Stone, II, 1000–1004, 1023–25, 1119–24, lists forty-four performances of *The Mayor of Garratt* in 1763 and thirty performances of *The Commissary* in 1765.
2. Belden, pp. 116–18.
2. Ibid., p. 115.
4. Ibid., pp. 115–16.
5. Trefman, appendix, pp. 275–81.
6. Fitzgerald, *Samuel Foote*, p. 230.
7. Belden, p. 116.
8. "Memoirs of Samuel Foote," *Bentley's Miscellany*, 1 (London, 1837), 305.
9. Willard Austin Kinne, *Revivals and Importations of French Comedies in England, 1749–1800* (New York, 1939), pp. 90–93.
10. Ibid., p. 92.
11. Cooke, *Memoirs*, II, 85–86.
12. *Boswell's Life of Johnson*, II, 299.
13. Ibid., IV, 333.

Chapter Eight

1. Belden, p. 125.
2. Ibid., p. 125.
3. Cooke, *Memoirs*, II, 66.
4. Ibid., 67.
5. Belden, p. 126.
6. Ibid., p. 128.
7. Ibid., p. 127.
8. Ibid., p. 131.
9. Ibid., p. 132.
10. Ibid., p. 132. Belden quotes a review in the *Gentleman's Magazine*, 40 (Aug. 1770), 379.
11. Dedication to *Taste*, p. vi.
12. Trefman, pp. 170–71.

Chapter Nine

1. Belden, p. 141.
2. Badcock, pseud. "John Bee," edited the 1830 edition of Foote's plays. Belden, p. 139 summarizes the rumors about the origin and the results of the play.
3. Belden, p. 145.
4. Stone, III, 1556, quotes from the *Theatrical Intelligencer*.
5. Belden, p. 140.
6. W. K. Wimsatt, Jr., "Foote and a Friend of Boswell's: A Note on *The Nabob*," *Modern Language Notes*, 57 (1942), 325–35.
7. Belden, p. 150.
8. Ibid., pp. 151–52.
9. *A History of English Drama* (Cambridge, 1955), III, 175.
10. Cooke, *Memoirs*, I, 177–82.
11. Belden, p. 157.
12. *Piety in Pattens*, ed. Bogorad, p. 5.

Chapter Ten

1. Belden, p. 187.
2. This point is also made by Belden, p. 160.
3. John Drinkwater, *Charles James Fox* (London, 1928), p. 22.
4. Bogorad, ed., *Piety in Pattens*, p. 58, glosses "Blossom" or "bloss" as slang terms for whore, citing J. Badcock, *Slang, A Dictionary of the Turf, the Ring . . .* (London, 1823).
5. James Boaden, *Memoirs of Mrs. Siddons*, 2 vols. (London, 1827), I, 61–64. Boaden names Gagahan as the original of Aircastle and reprints his character of Foote. Belden, p. 160, also fails to see the resemblance.
6. Belden, p. 187.
7. See chapter 6, p. 87.
8. Belden, pp. 161–64. I have followed Belden's account of these incidents.
9. Ibid., p. 162. Belden cites several reports of the new scene, which was advertised for June 19, 1776.
10. The details of the Sheridan–Linley romance are taken from E. M. Butler, *Sheridan: A Ghost Story* (London, 1931), pp. 158–78.
11. Butler, p. 175, speaks of her "sweetness of nature and delicate charm."
12. For example, *The World Displayed; or, a Curious Collection of Voyages and Travels*, published by John Newbery in 20 volumes (1759–1761; 1774–1778; 1790).
13. Elizabeth Mavor, *The Virgin Mistress, A Study in Survival: The Life of the Duchesss of Kingston* (London, 1964), p. 54. Details of Elizabeth

Chudleigh's life are taken from Mavor. A portrait of Miss Chudleigh as Iphigenia is reproduced in T. H. White, *The Age of Scandal*, foll. p. 120.

14. Mavor discusses the Rome visit and the preparations for the trial in chap. 6, pp. 112–31.

15. Belden, p. 39.

16. In his letter to the Lord Chamberlain, August 4, 1775. See Trefman, p. 239.

17. See Belden, p. 40ff., and Trefman, p. 236ff.

18. Belden, p. 46. Stuart's remarks on Jackson's character are in Lucyle Werkmeister, "Notes for a Revised Life of William Jackson," *Notes and Queries*, 206 (February, 1961), 43–47.

19. *Gentleman's Magazine*, 45 (Aug. 1775), 391–92. The correspondence was widely reprinted. See Belden, p. 43.

20. Cooke, *Memoirs*, I, 231–32.

21. Trefman, pp. 262–65, gives a lengthy account of Foote's illness and death.

Chapter Eleven

1. Cooke, *Memoirs*, III, 104–5.

2. Edward H. Weatherly, "Foote's revenge on Churchill and Lloyd," suggests that Foote did not greatly alter *Fatal Constancy*, which was itself a parody of heroic tragedy.

3. Printed in Tate Wilkinson, *The Wandering Patentee*, I, 295–96.

4. Ibid., p. 294.

5. Ibid., p. 298.

6. Ibid., p. 286.

7. *Theatre Survey*, 14, no. 1a (Fall, 1973).

8. George Speaight, *The History of the English Puppet Theatre* (London, 1955), pp. 111–13

9. Bogorad, in his commentary, pp. 61–97, reprints the pertinent reviews, letters, theatrical "puffs," and verses occasioned by the first performance and the subsequent revised versions.

10. Quoted in Bogorad, p. 80.

11. Genest, *Some Account of the English Stage*, V, 374–75. Bogorad, p. 52, notes that this part of the address, omitted from the printed versions of the exordium, appears in all the reviews and accounts of the first performance.

12. Wharton, "Satire and Panegyric in the Plays of Samuel Foote," p. 115.

13. *Morning Chronicle and London Advertiser*, March 19, 1773, quoted in Bogorad, p. 86.

14. *The Drama of Sensibility* (Gloucester, Mass., 1958), p. 244.

15. Belden, p. 176.

16. Tate Wilkinson, *The Wandering Patentee*, I, 291.
17. Ibid., p. 292.

Chapter Twelve

1. *Boswell's Life of Johnson*, II, 95, n. 2.
2. *Memoirs*, II, 49–50.
3. *Piety in Pattens*, p. 4.
4. *Memoirs*, II, 50.
5. *English Actors from Shakespeare to Macready*, 2 vols. (New York, 1879), I, 256.
6. Belden, pp. 190–91, gives an account of those who borrowed from Foote.
7. John Fyvie, "Samuel Foote," in *Wits, Beaux, and Beauties of the Georgian Era* (London, 1909), p. 60.

Selected Bibliography

PRIMARY SOURCES

1. Plays

Taste. London, 1752.
The Englishman in Paris. London, 1753.
The Knights. London, 1754.
The Englishman Return'd from Paris. London, 1756.
The Author. London, 1757.
The Minor. London, 1760.
The Orators. London, 1762.
The Mayor of Garret [Garratt]. London, 1763.
The Lyar. London, 1764.
The Patron. London, 1764.
The Commissary. London, 1765.
The Lame Lover. London, 1770.
The Maid of Bath. London, 1771. A corrupt text. First authorized edition, Colman's, London, 1778.
The Bankrupt. London, 1776.
The Devil Upon Two Sticks. London, 1778.
The Nabob. London, 1778.
The Cozeners. London, 1778.
A Trip to Calais. London, 1778.
The Capuchin. London, 1778.
The Diversions of the Morning, Second Act. In Tate Wilkinson's *Wandering Patentee.* York, 1795. Also in Cooke's *Memoirs of Samuel Foote* (London, 1805).
Tragedy a-la-Mode. In Tate Wilkinson's *Wandering Patentee.* York, 1795.
The Trial of Samuel Foote Esq. for a Libel on Peter Paragraph. In Tate Wilkinson's *Wandering Patentee.* York, 1795. Also in Cooke's *Memoirs* (London, 1805).
An Occasional Prelude Performed at the Opening of the Theatre Royal in The Haymarket, 1767. First printed entire in *Monthly Mirror*, 1804. Also in Cooke's *Memoirs* (London, 1805).

153

Samuel Foote's Primitive Puppet-Shew Featuring Piety in Pattens: A Critical Edition. Edited by Samuel N. Bogorad and Robert Gale Noyes. *Theatre Survey,* 14, no. 1a (Fall, 1973). Includes both the Folger Shakespeare Library and the Huntington Library manuscript versions of *Piety in Pattens,* carefully annotated, with a useful introduction. A pattern for future critical editions.

2. Collected Editions

The Works of Samuel Foote, Esq. 2 vols. London, 1799.
The Dramatic Works of Samuel Foote. 2 vols. London, 1809; reprint ed., New York: Benjamin Blom, 1968. Vol. 1 contains a brief *Life,* and *Taste, The Englishman in Paris, The Author, The Englishman Return'd from Paris, The Knights, The Mayor of Garratt, The Orators, The Minor, The Lyar,* and *The Patron.* Vol. 2 contains *The Commissary, The Lame Lover, The Bankrupt, The Cozeners, The Maid of Bath, The Nabob, The Devil Upon Two Sticks, A Trip to Calais,* and *The Capuchin.*
The Dramatic Works of Samuel Foote, With Remarks on each Play and an Essay on the Life, Genius, and Writings of the Author. Edited by John Bee (pseud. of John Badcock.) 3 vols. London, 1830. Contains the plays listed in the 1809 edition, and *The Diversions of the Morning, Second Act.*

3. Essays, Letters, and Translations

Apology for the Minor in a Letter to the Rev. Mr. Baine. Edinburgh, 1771.
The Comic Theatre . . . By Samuel Foote, Esq. and Others. 5 vols. London, 1762. Foote contributed a preface and a translation of *The Young Hypocrite.*
A Letter from Mr. Foote to the Reverend Author of the "Remarks, Critical and Christian," on the Minor. London, 1760. Also in Cooke's *Memoirs* (London, 1805).
The Roman and English Comedy Consider'd and Compar'd. London, 1747.
A Treatise on the Passions, so far as they regard the Stage. London, [1747]; reprint ed., New York: Benjamin Blom, 1971.

SECONDARY SOURCES

ANON. "Memoirs of Samuel Foote." *Bentley's Miscellany,* 1 (1837), 298–305. Commends Foote's pungent malicious humor, his originality, and his excellence in characterization but criticizes the poor construction of his plays, especially the weakness of his plots.
ANON. "On the Neglect of Foote as a Dramatic Writer." *Blackwood's Magazine,* 9 (April, 1821), 39–42. Praises Foote's "moral satire" and the

ease and elegance of his diction, and ascribes the neglect of Foote in part to Johnson's low opinion of his works.

ANON. *Wit for the Ton! The Convivial Jester; or, Sam Foote's last Budget Opened.* London, [1777?]. A tribute to Foote written soon after his death, which includes an assessment of his work and a collection of anecdotes and witticisms attributed to Foote.

BATTESTIN, MARTIN C. "Fielding and 'Master Punch' in Panton Street." *Philological Quarterly*, 45 (January, 1966), 191–208. Discusses Foote's mimicry of Henry Fielding in his *Auction of Pictures* (1748), and Fielding's retaliation.

BELDEN, MARY MEGIE. *The Dramatic Work of Samuel Foote.* Yale Studies in English, no. 80. New Haven, Conn.: Yale University Press, 1929; reprint ed., New York: Archon, 1970. A detailed scholarly treatment of the plays. Belden identifies a large number of the persons on whom Foote based his characters.

BEVIS, RICHARD W., ed. *Eighteenth Century Drama: Afterpieces.* London: Oxford University Press, 1970. Contains an introductory note on afterpiece drama and several examples of the genre, including Foote's *The Commissary.*

Bon Mots of Samuel Foote and Theodore Hook. Edited by Walter Jerrold, with grotesques by Aubrey Beardsley. London: Dent, 1894. An amusing collection of Footeana.

BOSWELL, JAMES. *Boswell's Life of Johnson.* Edited by George B. Hill, revised and enlarged L. F. Powell. 2d ed. 6 vols. Oxford: Oxford University Press, 1964. Contains Johnson's contradictory but entertaining opinions about Foote's character and dramatic abilities.

CLARKE, CHARLES COWDEN. "On the Comic Writers of England, No. 12– Foote and Farce-Writers." *The Gentleman's Magazine*, n.s. 8 (1872), 303–24. A rather digressive treatment of Foote, interesting for its recognition of the merits of farce, which Clarke sees as comedy exaggerated in all its features.

COOKE, WILLIAM. *Memoirs of Samuel Foote.* 3 vols. London: Richard Phillips, 1805. The earliest biography. Cooke knew Foote well but is not wholly uncritical of his friend. Contains a selection of Foote's witticisms, and the playlets *The Diversions of the Morning, Second Act, An Occasional Prelude,* and *The Trial of Samuel Foote.*

CORNER, BETSY C. "Dr. Melchisedech Broadbrim and the playwright." *Journal of the History of Medicine*, 7 (1952), 122–35. Identifies the original of Dr. Melchisedech Broadbrim, the Quaker physician in *The Devil Upon Two Sticks* as Dr. John Fothergill and discusses the aspects of medicine satirized by Foote.

FITZGERALD, PERCY H. *Samuel Foote, A Biography.* London: Chatto, 1910. A chatty and readable, though somewhat inaccurate biography.

FORSTER, JOHN. "Samuel Foote." In *Historical and Biographical Essays.*

SAMUEL FOOTE

2 vols. London: John Murray, 1858. The first modern treatment. Forster is generous in his praise of Foote's wit and skill in delineating
character while recognizing that his plays lack the plot development
necessary for first-rate comedy.

FYVIE, JOHN. "Samuel Foote." *Wits, Beaux, and Beauties of the Georgian
Era*. London: John Lane, the Bodley Head, 1909. An entertaining
biographical essay.

GENEST, JOHN. *Some Account of the English Stage*. 10 vols. Bath, 1882.
References to Foote by a contemporary. Much of the material in Genest is more easily located in *The London Stage*.

The London Stage: 1660–1800, Part 3, *1729–1747*. Edited by Arthur H.
Scouten. 2 vols. Carbondale, Illinois: Southern Illinois University
Press, 1961. *The London Stage* is an indispensable reference work.
Scouten's introduction includes a lucid exposition of the origin and
effects of the Licensing Act, and of the theatrical milieu at the begin-
ning of Foote's career.

The London Stage: 1660–1800, Part 4, *1747–1776*. Edited by George Winchester Stone, Jr. 3 vols. Carbondale, Illinois: Southern Illinois University Press, 1962. The introductory sections contain a brilliant and
detailed account of theatrical conditions during the Garrick era.

PRICE, CECIL. *Theatre in the Age of Garrick*. Oxford: Basil Blackwell,
1973. A useful study of theatrical conditions during Foote's career.

SCOUTEN, ARTHUR H. "On the Origin of Foote's matinees." *Theatre Notebook*, 7 (1953), 28–31. Points out that Foote did not truly invent the
matinee custom, but adapted it, as prize fights, public breakfastings,
and auctions of pictures were customarily held at noon.

SHERBO, ARTHUR. *English Sentimental Drama*. East Lansing, Mich.:
Michigan State University Press, 1957. A thoughtful and perceptive
treatment of sentimental drama.

STEVENSON, LLOYD G. "The Siege of Warwick Lane." *Journal of the History of Medicine*, 7 (1952), 105–21. Discusses the dispute between the
Fellows and Licentiates of the Royal College of Physicians, satirized
by Foote in *The Devil Upon Two Sticks*.

TREFMAN, SIMON. "Arthur Murphy's Long Lost *Englishman from Paris*:
A Manuscript Discovered." *Theatre Notebook*, 20 (Summer, 1966),
137–41. Discovery of Murphy's play proves that Foote's *Englishman
Return'd from Paris* was not plagiarized from Murphy, and is in fact
the better play.

———. *Sam Foote, Comedian, 1720–1777*. New York: New York University
Press, 1971. The only modern treatment of Foote's life. Trefman discusses the plays in the context of mid-eighteenth-century social and
theatrical history.

WEATHERLY, EDWARD H. "Foote's revenge on Churchill and Lloyd."
Huntington Library Quarterly, 9 (1945), 49–60. Identifies Foote's re-

character of the man responsible for the attack on Foote's reputation. Jackson apparently was not secretary to the Duchess of Kingston (satirized as Lady Kitty Crocodile in *A Trip to Calais*) but his malicious hounding of Foote gained him a generous reward from the Duchess.

WHARTON, ROBERT VERNER. "The Divided Sensibility of Samuel Foote." *Educational Theatre Journal*, 17 (1965), 31–37. Claims most students of Foote see him as a wit, mimic, and master of topical satire, and ignore a substantial vein of sentimentalism in his comedies.

WILKINSON, JOHN WELLS. "The Life and Works of Samuel Foote. Part One." 5 typescript vols. British Museum Cup.504.b.5. Copies are also in the Huntington Library and the University of Bristol Library. 1936. A carefully documented collection of materials pertaining to Foote's early life, Wilkinson's work is the essential reference for a scholarly biography.

WILKINSON, TATE. *The Wandering Patentee*. 4 vols. York, 1795. Wilkinson, a noted mimic, knew Foote well. Reprints *The Diversions of the Morning, Second Act, Tragedy a-la-Mode,* and *The Trial of Samuel Foote*.

WIMSATT, W. K., JR. "Foote and a Friend of Boswell's: A Note on *The Nabob*." *Modern Language Notes*, 57 (1942), 325–35. Suggests several persons Foote may have satirized in *The Nabob*, concluding that the portrait was a composite.

WOOD, CHRISTOPHER. "An Eighteenth-Century Satire on the Art Market." *Connoisseur*, 163 (1966), 240–42. Discusses Foote's satire in *Taste*.

Index